JAMES
The Incredible Number 10

D1073679

JAMES

The Incredible Number 10

By

Michael Part

Sole
BOOKS

A special thank you to Yonatan, Yaron, and Guy Ginsberg
Cover design: Omer Pikarski
Front cover picture: Reuters - Andrea Comas
Back cover picture: Reuters - Juan Medina
ZIL - Tags: Soccer Sport World Cup
Series editor: Y Ginsberg
Page layout design: Lynn M. Snyder
Library of Congress Cataloging-in-Publication data available.

ISBN 978-1-938591-38-9
E-ISBN 978-1-938591-39-6

Published by Sole Books, Beverly Hills, California
Printed in the United States of America
First edition September 2016
10 9 8 7 6 5 4 3 2 1

www.solebooks.com

To my mentor and brother from another mother,
Steven E. de Souza

Chapter One

"I NEVER DREAMED OF BECOMING A PROFESSIONAL SOCCER PLAYER," James Rodriguez said. "But I guess I was destined to be one from the day I was born."

The Reporter wrote furiously into his notebook while James pulled on his cleats and straightened his socks. It was a training day, just a couple days before the last 16 round match with Uruguay and the press was hounding him. He had already scored three goals in this 2014 World Cup, the most in the tournament.

The reporter chuckled. "I'm ready to listen, James. I want to hear it all," he said. He pronounced his name correctly, the way it was pronounced in Colombia: *Ha-mez.*

James flashed a big smile.

The reporter had scored bigtime getting a one-on-one interview with James Rodriguez before the big match against Uruguay. James himself invited him in to the Colombian national dressing room. It was an honor to be anywhere close to the great *Los Cafeteros,* the People of the Coffee, the nickname of the Colombian National Team. The Reporter straddled the bench opposite the star midfielder, writing furiously into his notepad, getting down every word James said. "This is great stuff," the reporter muttered, scribbling on a notebook page, then turning the page and continuing to write, never missing a beat.

The room was noisy and Abel Aguilar, James' midfield partner on the team, trotted by and smacked him on the back of his head, then turned to the reporter. "You know who you're talking to? That's *El Nuevo Pibe!* Ask Valderrama! He said so himself!" He laughed and headed for the door on the other side of the room. "Three goals in three matches!"

The Reporter turned back to James. "Carlos Valderrama is *El Pibe…* the kid… and he himself said you were his successor three years ago after you played in the U20. Do you agree?"

"That's for you to say, not me," James blushed and fought to get the words out. It still happened sometimes whenever he was nervous — or embarrassed.

"I'll get you for this, Abel!" He shouted back.

James' agent, Jorge Mendes, told him he needed to learn how to take a compliment, but his mother Pilar and stepfather Juancar, had always taught him to be humble and he was never comfortable with all the praise. He knew he had to keep his pride in check. Juancar always said, "Any more pride than pride in your work, is too much pride." Well, this was pride in work, right? So it must be okay.

Every fan in Colombia knew that James Rodriguez was one of the key players to lift Colombia to the World Cup. In every World Cup, a new star is born, and since the start of the Brazil tournament, all eyes were on him.

He was Man of the Match in their first game against Greece, where he scored in the 90th minute. He was Man of the Match in their second game against Ivory Coast, where he scored another goal and another in their 4–1 victory over Japan where he scored in the 90th. He felt like he had barely gotten started, but he caused quite a stir in the world media and around the numerous World Cup pitches in Brazil, rising up from cities like Belo Horizonte, Brasilia, and Cuiaba, where the first three Colombian matches were played.

In the round of 16, James' beloved Colombian national team was bound to play against the great team from Uruguay. He felt anxious. As usual. But he always knew, when he felt anxious before a match, it would disappear when his feet hit the grass and he touched the ball.

James knew that his friend calling him *El Nuevo Pibe* was paying him the supreme compliment. *El Pibe,* the kid, was a legend of the game of soccer in various South American countries. In Argentina, *El Pibe* was Maradona. In Colombia, it was Carlos Valderrama, one of the country's greatest players. When Valderrama proclaimed him *El Pibe,* he almost fainted. He had had a lot of weird dreams over the years, especially when he was a kid, but he never dreamed he would follow Carlos Valderrama.

James read all sorts of things about himself: stuff like he was destined to be Colombia's greatest player. That kind of talk kept him up at night and made him choose his words carefully. He hesitated for a moment then realized that whatever he wanted to talk about, would come out just fine.

"What do you want to know?" He finally asked the Reporter.

The Reporter grinned. *"Everything."* The men shared a laugh. "Let's start with your first memory of soccer."

James though about it. Was it the real memory or something his mom told him that forever was engraved in his memory?

It happened in Cucuta, the city where he was born. He was just two years old.

They were at *General Santander Stadium.* His father, Wilson, was out on the field dressed in the black and red of Cucuta Deportivo, the pro team, training with the rest of the squad. His mother was in the stands and little baby James sat next to her. He wanted to go down on the field. Sitting still drove him crazy. His mother said he was always like that. In fact, he came into this world, kicking and flailing.

He was born on the 12th of July, 1991. Cúcuta, Colombia, is a city on the Colombian and Venezuelan border in the eastern branch of the Colombian Andes. His mother's name was Maria del Pilar Rubio Rodriguez and his father was Wilson James Rodriguez Bedolla.

On the day he was born, it was scorching hot and raining. Typical weather for July in Cucuta. During labor, baby James kicked up a storm and it hurt as his mom and dad raced in their old car across town to the Socorro Medico Santa Fe Pediatric Clinic in the Occidental area of Cucuta.

"He's face up!" The doctor exclaimed when James finally came out.

Usually, babies come out belly down. "He's not facing the net," Pilar mumbled. She was such a huge soccer fan, she tended to relate everything to a sort of soccer field of life, so her outburst was not unexpected. When her son grew up she would later wonder jokingly if his coming out upside-down had something to do with how he did not have to face the net to score a goal.

Years later, his mother told him that he squirmed and wiggled and flailed his arms and legs like an octopus of runaway fire hoses and was as slippery as a river eel, and that if he could do that on the pitch, he could escape any defense.

His mother took him to matches and practices and while she watched her striker husband, Wilson, play, James squirmed and could not sit still.

Most games, he wore a toddler version of the red and black Deportivo jersey his father wore. He pointed his two-year-old index finger down at the field where the team was warming up.

"Okay," his mother said. "Walk — don't run."

James nodded and took off.

He raced down the stairs and charged out on the field without missing a step.

Pilar held her breath his whole way down, counting the rows until he hit solid ground.

James ran along the sideline as the Deportivo squad did their warmups. He imitated every move his father made. If Wilson turned left, James faded left. If Wilson spun around, James spun around. If

Wilson went down, James went down. And when his father kicked the ball—

James kicked an imaginary ball with such unbridled enthusiasm, the momentum sent him flying in the air. He flailed his arms and legs like the day he was born, and slammed into the ground.

Pilar leaped to her feet.

James looked up, trying not to cry. All the men on his father's team had stopped what they were doing. His father trotted over and picked him up by the back of his shirt and stood him up again. "That would've been some kick!" Wilson said and chuckled. "I didn't know you were a lefty!"

James grinned, not having a clue what his papa meant.

The Deportivo players laughed and the laughter washed over him and took away the pain. He loved the sound of their laughter. Any laughter. He looked up at his father, blocking the sun, outlined in a halo of golden light. "Go back to your mama," his father said and went back to the team. They resumed their drills and suddenly his mother was there beside him, brushing him off and pulling him back into the stands where he would be safe again.

The moment was a twinkle in time that brought tears to his eyes whenever he remembered. It was so long ago. More than twenty years. It was almost like a dream.

He had but one picture his mother had given him that was dear to him and part of his earliest soccer memory. It was of his father, dressed in his Cucuta Deportivo uniform, the vast stands behind him in the background filled with over 40,000 fans waiting to see their team play. It had rained that day and the emerald grass at General Santander Stadium had grown overnight and needed mowing. It was of his father holding him in his arms.

And it was the only memory he had of his father when he was growing up.

Chapter Two

THREE-YEAR-OLD JAMES turned the big black pot over on its side on the kitchen floor and used it as a garage for his scrub-brush car. There were no toys in the house, other than his scuffed-up soccer ball that he always kept near him. He played in the kitchen because of the yelling in the other room. His mother and father yelled at each other a lot.

After a couple minutes, Wilson poked his head into the kitchen to check on him. James looked up and saw that his Papa's face was flush and his eyes were red.

"He's okay!" Wilson shouted to Pilar in the next room. "He's playing with the pots and pans!" Then he vanished back into the living room.

That night after supper, James tucked himself in. His father had gone out. When he heard his mother coming toward his room, he quickly closed his eyes. His mom tiptoed in and knelt beside the bed and kissed his forehead, thinking he was asleep. It grew quiet, so he opened one eye to see what was going on and she was still there, looking at him. He quickly re-closed his eye.

"You're trying to fool me Jamesito," she soothed, calling him by his nickname. "We should never, ever lie to each other."

James smiled and slowly opened his eyes. "Sorry, mama." She kissed him again on the forehead and he asked: "Are you mad at me for playing with the pots and pans?"

"Of course not," she replied.

Her face softened. James was everything to her. She gently stroked his cheek and he closed his eyes and grew drowsy. "You have a wonderful imagination, mijo," she said. "But you will have real toys soon enough."

"When?" James asked sleepily.

"When we go home to Ibague. Your uncles will make sure you have toys to play with and I can get back to cooking in my pots and scrubbing with my brushes." She giggled and he did too.

"And papa too?" He asked.

She could not bring herself to respond and he drifted off.

Years later, while he watched his own daughter sleep, he remembered that night. It was one of the last peaceful nights of sleep they had for a very long time.

James felt someone shake him and he opened his eyes. It was still dark, but the sky was dark blue. He did not like getting up early and rolled over. His mother shook him again and this time he saw it was her. The sun was just coming up and he could already feel the heat through his thin blanket.

Pilar wordlessly helped him dress and he could see she was holding back the tears. A few minutes later, they were out the door with his father as the sun just crested the horizon. Wilson carried a new soccer ball. They walked silently up the street to his father's car. James walked between them. Then his mother pulled him to a stop and his father knelt down so he could be close to him. "Don't be like me," he whispered and handed him the ball. Then he took James by his shoulders and hugged him. James felt his heart beating in his chest like a runaway train and tried to speak. "B-bye, p-papa," was all he could say. No more words came out. Wilson kissed his son goodbye, took one last look at Pilar, then got in his car and drove away.

James watched the car go down the hill, make a turn, and disappear. He hoped his father would return, like he always did.

His mother stood beside him. He took her hand in his. "When P-a-pa will be b-b-ack," he stammered.

Pilar stared at him. She couldn't tell him the truth. Not now. She had not heard him stutter before. "Why are you talking like that?" She asked.

James looked away, embarrassed. He didn't know why. He just couldn't get the words out.

Pilar studied her son then let it be. She squeezed his hand. "Let's go home," she said softly. "We have to pack." Then she and three-year-old James walked back up the street to their little house and disappeared inside.

Chapter Three

JAMES AND HIS MOTHER MOVED TO IBAGUE. Although he moved around a lot in his youth, it was Ibague that he called his home. They lived with his grandmother and his uncles. And the first place his mother took him when they arrived, was the *Estadio Manuel Murillo Toro,* home of Club Deportivo Cooperamos Tolima.

Ibague was a soccer town, nestled at a little over 4000 feet in the Colombian Andes on a large pad of rain forest, 300 miles from Cúcuta and the Venezuelan border.

It was not long after they moved to Ibague that Pilar went to work as a secretary at the local cement factory. She walked home to Arkaparaiso every evening after the whistle blew and James always waited for her in the kitchen, watching through the window.

One day, when she walked home, she was not

alone. A man was with her. He was not too tall, but muscular and bald. They talked all the way to her front door, then he gave her the soccer ball he had been carrying, then continued on his way down the road.

Grandma Miriam, James, Mario, and Andrew, came in from the back and sat down at the table, their dinner plates in front of them.

When Pilar stepped into the kitchen, Miriam raised one eyebrow and gave her a look. "Where did you get the ball?"

Pilar blushed. "A friend," she replied. "From work." She shoved the ball at James. "It is for you, Jamesito."

"He's good, you know," Mario said.

"Oh?" Pilar asked. "Really?"

"We've been playing ball with the little one. He's got a mean left foot."

"I know," she said proudly. "I have eyes."

"It is in his blood," Mario said. "His uncle Arley is playing for Independiente Medellin and of course, there is his father—"

"Enough," Pilar said. "No need to bring him into it."

"Sorry," Mario said.

James did not know what they were talking about. He was busy bouncing the ball.

Nine months later he bounced it again in the exact same place, just as he did every day from then until now except now the ball was scuffed and looked like it had been played every day for all that time. "Put the ball down, Jamesito," Pilar said, turning from the stove with a plate of chicken Arepas. Grandma Miriam sat across from him and grinned at him. Arepas were a Venezuelan dish of corn griddle cakes wrapped around spicy chicken and avocado. "Eat," Pilar said, picking up the children's history book.

James ate while Pilar read. "Ibague was founded in 1550 by the Spanish conquistador, Andres Lopez Galarza," Pilar said, turning the page. "Galarza thought the Amerindian native population, known as the Panches, who lived on both sides of the Magdalena River, were not only fierce warriors... but cannibals." She turned her face toward him and opened her mouth and hissed like a vampire.

"Aaaah!" James blurted out. "You s-scared m-me!"

"Pilar!" Miriam scolded. "You frightened him!"

"I'm scaring the words out of him," she said, chuckling, ruffling his hair.

"I t-thought t-they were s-soccer players!" He said and giggled.

James did not say much these days so it was fun getting him to talk. It was a year since they moved to the Highlands of Ibague, to the Arkaparaiso neighborhood. His stutter had become a part of him in that year after his father left them. The doctors said it was rare that it came to him so young as stuttering usually did not show up until at least age seven.

For James, talking was a nuisance and he constantly had to work around it. In fact, it was easier to just say nothing and remain silent. It felt safe. However, when it was just him and his mom, he talked.

Pilar gently brushed his cheek. "Everything with you is soccer, eh?" she asked.

"You t-too," he quipped and his grin melted her heart. He was everything to her and if truth be told, she loved soccer just as much as he did.

He grabbed his ball and was about to go outside.

"Where do you think *you're* going?" She asked.

"Banquitas," he said, "P-pickup game!" He shouted as he let the screen door go and charged off up the street.

"Don't forget to— ", she said. The screen door slammed shut and he was gone.

"— drink!"

"I think he's smart enough to know when to drink," Miriam grinned. "You worry too much."

Pilar bit her lip and nodded. "You're right. I'll have Mario check up on him."

James let the ball drop to the road and kept it close to his left foot as he walked up the hill, dribbling as he went, shifting the ball from one foot to the other, never losing it. The futsal court was a block away and was on a small piece of land that separated the Valparaiso from Las Palmeras neighborhoods. It also doubled as a basketball court. There were permanent lines drawn for futsal and temporary lines for basketball. The futsal goals were under the net less basketball hoops. For four-year-old James, he seemed to be the only one who cared about basketball and in between pickups, and liked to shoot hoops with his scuffed-up soccer ball. He was good at it.

"Ha-mezzzzz!!" The boys from the Valparaiso side, his side, shouted and greeted him like a brother. They needed him even though he was a full two years younger than all of them. The regular neighborhood four-a-side pick-up match had just begun and the boys from neighboring Las Palmeras had already scored.

Banquitas was a Columbian version of Futsal: small court, small squad and small goals. The court was surrounded by tall houses with balconies, so there was always an audience watching the games.

As soon as the neighbors heard the noisy boys below, they knew a match had begun and poured out onto their balconies to watch. Soccer was the number one entertainment in the neighborhood.

Everyone loved the beautiful game.

James' uncles, Mario and Andrew were already there, watching from the sidelines and acting as refs and coaches whenever the boys started screaming at each other.

James was the youngest player on the pitch. All the kids were at least a couple years older. When he moved to Ibague last year, his uncles took him under their wing and showed him how to play ball. But he was a fast learner and before long, he was showing *them* how to play.

James left his ball on the sideline and raced onto the court. The first thing he did was look up to see who was watching. All the balconies of the casitas surrounding the asphalt pitch were filled with kids and moms and dads.

He loved playing the game. It was the most exciting feeling he ever had in his entire life. Running around, kicking and scoring. He was fast and he could score. And when he scored, he loved the cheers. It made him want to score even more.

After the game, James walked home with the ball under his arm, an uncle on either side of him. Mario grinned at his nephew. "You live with that ball, don't you?" He asked.

He nodded, and when he got home, his mother immediately saw the happiness in his eyes. He asked her if he could keep doing it tomorrow, and the day after tomorrow and the day after that.

She smiled and kissed him. "As long as it makes you happy," she said.

Chapter Four

JAMES SAT IN FRONT OF THE TV and leaned his back against the chair. He was more comfortable on the floor with his ball within reach. His favorite show was just coming on.

Captain Tsubasa. It was a cartoon show that aired a new episode every day. In Japan, where the show originated, it was known as an *Anime*.

The hero of the series, in Spanish, was known as *Oliver Atom.* In Japanese he was Tsubasa Ozora and when he was promoted to lead his soccer team to victory, he became known as *Captain Tsubasa.* The story went, Oliver and his mother moved to a new city and he joined a new soccer team. He lived mostly alone with his mother because his father, Koudai, was a sea captain and was always gone. But someday, the story told, Oliver's father would return.

James had the same wish.

Pilar brought him a tray with a glass of goat's milk and a sandwich and set it down on the floor and he snatched up the sandwich and munched it. "Are all papas bad, m-mama?" he asked between bites.

"Of course not, mijo," Pilar replied.

"I-I'm not gonna be bad," he said, never taking his eyes off the screen.

Pilar knelt down and snuggled him. "Don't worry. That won't be for you to decide. It will be up to God," she soothed.

He grinned at her and gave her a hug. "I-I just need you," he said.

On the TV, Oliver Atom and his team went to Uruguay and won the match.

One day, while he was watching his favorite show on TV, Pilar poked her head out of the kitchen and grinned at her son. "Hey, someone's coming over I want you to meet."

"Okay," James nodded.

A man he saw before came into the room. He was the one who gave his mother the soccer ball she gave to him. His name was Juan Carlos

Restrepo. Everyone called him Juancar. He worked with his mom and was the company's transportation manager. He was kind and smart. He also happened to be an engineer, and more importantly, soccer crazy. He walked his mother home every day from work but never came into the house. But today was different. He came in.

Juancar walked right in from the kitchen and plunked himself down on the sofa next to James.

"Hey," Juancar said and checking out the TV screen. "Oliver Atom! My favorite show!"

James, who kept his soccer ball at his feet, scooted to the other end of the sofa, away from him, bringing the ball with him. He gave the stranger a look. Actually, it was more of a glare. "W-who are you?"

Juancar grinned. "I'm the one who gave you that ball," he said and shoved out his hand. "My name is Juan Carlos, but you can call me Juancar. I work with your mother. "He took James' hand and shook it. "I hear that you are the man of the house."

James cocked his head and nodded. "Y-yes," he said. He liked that this man called him a man.

Pilar came in with a tray of glasses of lemonade. "Oh good, I see you two are getting to know each other," she said, setting the drinks down on the table, handing one to Juancar. James grabbed it first and quickly took a gulp to claim it as his own.

Juancar grinned at Pilar but she was not thrilled. "James, that was very rude," she scolded. "You know we always serve guests first. Now apologize"

"No, it's fine, Pilar," Juancar said.

"No it's not," she replied. "Go on, James. Say something."

James studied the strange, mysterious man he's been seeing out the window for months, the man who liked Oliver Atom, but he said nothing. Juancar then pointed to the ball. "Nice ball," he said. "Must have been a great man who gave that to you." He laughed.

James gave him a look then expertly flicked it to him.

Juancar was ready and caught the ball with his ankle and trapped it. "Let's go to the park," Juancar said, grabbing the ball and heading for the door. Pilar was already waiting at the door. He took her hand with his other hand. "You too," he said.

James flashed a smile.

When Juancar and Pilar got outside, he dropped the ball and dribbled it as he walked along the dirt road, holding Pilar's hand. James caught up to them and Juancar flicked it to him. "Who do you play for?" Juancar asked.

"Arkaparaiso," James said.

"Yeah, I think I know where that is," Juancar said.

"You better!" James giggled. "It's right here!"

"Oh yeah," Juancar said. "I must've forgot."

"Who do *you* play for?" James asked, passing the ball a with his left foot directly to Juancar.

"I'm too old," Juancar said. "But a long time ago, I played for Atletico Nacional in Medellin." He kicked the ball back to the boy. "Perhaps you've heard of me."

"Nope." He left-footed it back to him.

"That's a nice left foot you got there," Juancar said.

"Yeah, I can kick with both," James replied, wriggling his right foot. They arrived at the park and the pitch at the top of the hill. It was empty. Juancar dropped the ball and flicked it to the boy. "Let's play. See if you can get past me."

James captured the ball and dribbled around Juancar moving the ball from right to left.

"Like that?" He asked.

Juancar took a moment to process what he had just seen, then put his hands on his hips and gave the boy a broad grin: "Can you do it faster"

James did it again. Faster.

"Like that?" he said after he finished the dribble with a strong left kick.

"Perfect," Juancar said smiling. "You are really good."

Chapter Five

"YOU ARE RIGHT ABOUT THAT LEFT FOOT," Juancar remarked to Pilar. "Too bad he doesn't have two of them."

James zig-zagged down the field like he was avoiding imaginary defenders and rocketed the ball into the goal with his right foot.

"Actually, he does," Pilar said, grinning.

Just then the ball came sailing over Pilar's head and landed at Juancar's feet. James was not even looking when he kicked it. Juancar picked it up and threw it at James' and James controlled it.

"How does he do that?" Juancar asked, amazed.

"Magic," Pilar said proudly.

James spread his arms straight out on either side of him then bent them back until they were slightly behind him and wiggled his fingers. "I still see my fingers," he said.

"Oh my God," Juancar marveled. "You've got

super peripheral vision!"

James kicked the ball over them and followed it. "W-what's t-that?" He asked.

"You can see more than other kids can see."

"I do?"

"Yes you do. And that can help you become a great player. You love the game, don't you?" Juancar asked.

"Y-yeah," James said. He could feel the words getting jumbled up and told himself to slow down.

"You want to be a pro?"

James shook his head. "N-no, I – I just want to w-win." He felt flustered.

Juancar draped his arm over the boy's shoulders. "Relax, you can talk any way you want. I *like* the way you talk."

James blushed and looked at the ground. Juancar dropped the ball and flicked it to him. "Let's go get a snack," he said. James nodded, bounced the ball with his feet to his hand and started back toward home.

Juancar draped his arm over Pilar's shoulders.

James walked behind them and heard everything

they said.

"He needs to go to the soccer academy," Juancar said.

"But that is way too expensive," Pilar argued.

"Just the same," Juancar said. "I want to find him a place to go," he said.

"But he says he doesn't want to be a player," Pilar said although she wished James would love the idea.

"Why not? All boys want to be soccer players. He'll change his mind."

James charged ahead of them, dribbling the ball on the road to home and Juancar shook his head in wonder. "Look at him. Four years old and he has a fire in him. He's like a bull."

"A very skinny bull," Pilar joked.

Juancar chuckled. "You're right. There's not much meat on him. We will have to do something about that."

"We?" Pilar asked. It was a hopeful question. She had been seeing Juan Carlos Restrepo for months.

Juancar looked at Pilar. "Yes, *we*," he replied. "You and I. And James."

Pilar smiled. For the first time in a long time, she felt safe again.

A month later, Juancar proposed marriage to Pilar and they were married in the local cathedral in Tolima. Juan Carlos Restrepo became James' stepfather and ever since, the three of them were inseparable.

The views from their yellow-fronted home in Arkaparaiso, in all directions, always included soccer, whether it was the stadium, the neighborhood pitch, or a pick-up game in the street. A few weeks later, from the second floor balcony, James watched the third division of Deportes Tolima play a friendly in the nearby stadium. Juancar had the day off and spent it with his stepson. "That's Jorge Luis Bernal," Juancar said, pointing at a man on the field. "He's the team's technical director. He could be great if he had a better squad."

James nodded, listening intently to his stepfather's every word as he talked about the history of Deportes Tolima and how lucky they were to see them play from their own balcony. When the match was over, James said: "Let's go downstairs, there's a match on TV."

They both started down the stairs, then Juancar stopped and James kept going. "Oh! I forgot something," Juancar said and bounded back up the stairs.

"It's almost on!" James shouted and raced to the couch and leaped over the back and plopped down on it, flicking the remote, turning on the television set.

Juancar came down the stairs carrying a shoebox.

"W-what's that?" James asked.

Juancar came over and gave the box to James, who tore it open. Inside, was a brand new pair of light-blue and white Adidas soccer cleats. James' eyes grew wide as he pulled a shoe out and put it on. It fit perfectly. Juancar plopped down on the couch next to him. "I figured it was time you had some decent shoes if you're going to continue to tear up the field."

James put his arms around Juancar's neck and hugged him.

A few moments later, a soccer match came on TV and both of them watched. Independiente Nacional was going for a penalty kick. James moved closer to his stepfather. "So, what does the man of the

house think about enrolling in the soccer academy?"
Juancar asked.

James smiled sleepily. "I'm not the man of the
house," he said. "You are."

Juancar smiled and draped his arm over the boy's
shoulders. James closed his eyes and went to sleep.

When Pilar walked home from the station after
work that day and reached the narrow walkway to
the front door, she could already hear the television
blaring from inside the house. The soccer match
was on and it was loud enough to wake the dead.
When she came through the door, she saw Juancar
slumbering on the couch and James asleep in his
arms. She tiptoed over to the TV and turned it down
and neither of them stirred, so she joined them on
the couch and closed her eyes and at that moment,
and all the other moments going forward, felt they
were a family again.

Chapter Six

ONE EVENING, Juancar came home upset. "I lost my job," he said.

James sensed that his mother and stepfather were worried.

But then, a week later, Juancar came home and cheerfully announced at the dinner table, "Great news! I have been offered a better job!"

Everyone was relieved and the entire family, Uncles, Grandma, and Pilar congratulated the newest addition to their family. They all liked Juancar. Even James smiled.

"That's fantastic!" Andrew said, patting Juancar on the back. "Doing the same thing?"

"Yes, it is an engineering job."

"Which company in Ibague is it?" Grandma Miriam asked, sipping her after-dinner coffee.

Juancar's eyes darted from his wife to the rest of the family around the table. "Well," he said. "The company is not exactly in Ibague..."

There was a long moment of silence. "Where exactly is it?" Miriam asked.

"Exactly speaking... my new job is in... Bogota," Juancar replied.

The silence of being underneath a thick blanket.

Bogota, the capital of Colombia, was over 120 miles away. But James did not yet realize what was about to happen. In a matter of days, his mother, his new stepfather, and himself would be leaving their tight-knit family to open a new chapter in their lives.

And so, when Grandma Miriam cried, James had no idea why, he just knew she was sad so he rushed into her arms and comforted her. He had never seen her cry before. It was strange and scary.

"Don't worry," Grandma whispered in his hear. "I cry because I love you."

Juancar drove the 120 miles to Bogota on Highway 40, which brought the family down to less than 1000 feet above sea level, through the city of Girardot, the lowest point of the trip, then back up into the Andes through La Serena and Fusagasuga and on to Bogota and almost 9000 feet above sea level. Because of the mountainous roads, the drive took all day. When Juancar drove up Avenida Calle 63 into the Salitre neighborhood of Bogota, he pointed out the botanical gardens on one side and *Salitre Magico,* the amusement park, on the other.

When they drove into their new neighborhood they passed the soccer academy. James bounced all over the backseat in excitement. Two teams were practicing on the pitch. One squad in orange and white and green and the other in red, all jerseys with the red and green Sporting Cristal emblem emblazoned on their chests.

One boy took a corner kick that went nowhere

"Did you see that kick?" James asked, pointing.

"That's the U7 squad," Juancar said, stopping the car. "I think they need your help." His eyes met his stepson's in the rearview mirror. "What do you think? Do you see yourself on that team?"

"M-me?" James said, his heart racing.

"It's not just a place to play soccer, it's an academy," Juancar said softly, noticing his stepson's anxiety.

"Y-you mean I can play here?" James asked, never taking his eyes off the kids on the pitch.

"Sure," Juancar shrugged. "If I have anything to say about it. You gotta play somewhere, right?"

James pressed his face against the window. He could not believe it. The place was huge.

"When?" James asked. "Now?"

His mom and stepdad laughed.

"First we need to get to our new home," his mom said.

"We'll come back tomorrow," Juancar promised.

They drove to their new home. For James, Salitre was nothing but parks and awesome places to play. For Pilar, however, it was another story.

"I can't breathe," she said, taking a deep breath and coughing, plopping into a chair at the dining table of their new home, crossing her arms and scowling.

James knew she was irritated because she always crossed her arms when she was upset.

Juancar came up behind her and rubbed her shoulders. "You'll get used to the altitude in a few days," he said, in a soothing voice.

James loved the new house, but there was only one thing on his mind: the soccer academy. He could not stop thinking about it.

The *Club Academia De Futbol Sporting Cristal,* known as *Sporting Cristal,* was situated on more than 20 acres of land between Calle 63c and 63a and up the road from the free university, the *Instituto Tecnico Industrial Francisco Jose De Caldas.* The academy included soccer pitches, a velodrome, a BMX course, a baseball diamond, tennis courts, and the Coliseo Cubierto El Salitre, an indoor professional basketball court.

And as he promised, the next day, Juancar took James to Sporting Cristal and signed him up.

Chapter Seven

THERE WERE A COUPLE OF REASONS why Juancar signed James up with Sporting Cristal. First, it was the only decent club around and he knew James was talented and needed a club. Second, over the thirty-something years the academy had been in existence in Salitre, the management always seemed to know a good player when they saw one.

Five minutes into the U7 tryout, the Cristal manager marched up to Juancar on the sideline and slapped him on the back. "He's in," he said then shook his head in wonderment. "Not even five years old! Amazing. I haven't seen a kid like him in a long time." Then he gave Juancar's broad shoulders a squeeze. "That's some left foot," he said and marched off.

"No kidding," Juancar said to himself. He stood on the sideline and grinned as Pilar joined him.

"What'd he say?" Pilar asked.

"He likes his left foot," he said to her, never taking his eyes off his stepson out on the field.

Pilar linked her arm in his. "Wait until he finds out he's got two of them," she said, and Juancar laughed.

There was something about the way the almost five-year-old handled the ball with his foot: the way he toed the ball, then handily shifted his touch from the inner edge to the outer edge and the way he controlled the ball. He knew, that with the right training, James could prove to be a prodigy.

A few months later, Pilar watched her son charge along the sideline of the La Morena soccer field, dribbling the ball from left to right from the inner to the outer side of his foot. Then he feigned left and the keeper dove right as he shifted to the outside of his left foot and slammed it into the left corner of the net, leaving the keeper staring at the ball as it rolled to the back of the net. Everyone cheered.

James' U7 squad had won the Bogota youth tournament.

Pilar burst into tears and left.

Juancar saw she was in distress and went after

her and found her leaning against their car in the
parking lot. He could barely console her. "I miss my
family," she sobbed.

He knew he had to do something.

"Come, the trophy ceremony is about to start."
Pilar, face streaked with tears, nodded.

A few moments later, James stood on the field
as his squad was handed the trophy for best youth
team in Bogota. James raised the trophy in the air
and everyone cheered. It was his first team and his
first win.

Pilar tried hard to be strong that day, but she
was lonely and her heart was breaking. She felt bad
when she told her husband behind the dressing
rooms while waiting for James that she could not
stay in Bogota any longer and wanted to go home to
Ibague.

When James came out of the dressing room
carrying his kit bag, beaming with pride from the
win, he saw his parents standing near the car. He
watched as Juancar leaned close to Pilar and he
heard them speaking softly. "I should have known
why you were so sad, Pilar," he said. "I'm sorry."

She looked up and saw James coming. "We'll talk about this later," she said, waving James over. "Congratulations! You were incredible!"

He hugged his mother, knowing exactly what to say. "I wish g-grandma and grandpa were here," he said and she hugged him tighter.

"How did you get so smart?" She asked.
His coach came out and headed for his car. "Congratulations, James!" He said.

"T-thanks, c-coach!" James replied.

The coach stopped in his tracks and gawked at him. "I don't believe it!" He said.

"Is something wrong?" Pilar asked.

"No, not at all. It's just that I've probably heard less than ten words out of him the whole time he's been here, and I haven't heard him say anything in weeks!"

"He likes to talk with his feet," Pilar said proudly.

"He's got a golden boot, that is for sure," the coach said, getting into his car, driving away.

On the way home, the three talked it out. "I get headaches every day. The doctor says it's the altitude." But it was more than that. Pilar missed her home in Ibague and the loneliness was tearing her apart inside.

After James went to bed that night, Juancar and Pilar had coffee in the kitchen. Juancar lit a candle. "Why don't you and James go back to Ibague," he said, taking her hand.

"No we won't leave you," Pilar insisted.

"You won't be leaving me. I think I can work it out to come home to Ibague every couple weeks, maybe even every weekend. I'll drive you two back and stay until I get James into a good academy there before I return to Bogota. Settle him into a good education."

"But there's just Campestre and it is so expensive!"

"Trust me," he said. "I can make it work."

Tears filled Pilar's eyes and she took his hand in both of hers and kissed it. "You are truly a gift from God."

Juancar hugged her. He wanted Pilar and James to be happy. And he had big plans for his stepson.

The next day, Pilar and James said goodbye to Bogota and made their way back to Ibague.

Chapter Eight

THE *Corporación Club Campestre de Ibagué*
was a soccer club wrapped inside an exclusive
country club in the Highlands of Ibague. It was
fancy and prestigious, but it did not have much of
a winning youth team. They also did not let just
anyone join the youth team, especially if the parents
were not members, and Juancar and Pilar were
definitely not members. So, when Juancar offered
them James Rodriguez to play for them, they turned
him down without even a tryout.

It would turn out to be the *only* time a team
turned him down.

Yul Brinner Calderon walked around the Jordan
neighborhood of Ibague near where James and
his family lived and put up posters advertising his
soccer school in all the shop windows. He knew the
shop owners and they let him use their window.
His sign was simple and read: *"SPORT CLUB.*

PH. 2689636." It included a picture of the youth
team's uniform of yellow and blue, similar to the
Columbian national team's uniforms. He figured
it would attract the kids and they would tell their
parents and the parents would sign the kid up
and he could pay the club's bills. They needed the
money badly.

Juancar left Club Campestre disappointed after
they rejected James without even seeing him play.
On his way home, he walked through Jordan and
saw Yul Calderon stapling a bright yellow poster for
his school on a telephone pole.

"What is this club you are talking about?" He asked.

Calderon eyeballed Juancar for a split second to
size him up. After all this work of raising money,
putting up posters and managing a team, there was
no sense in talking to someone about joining if they
weren't serious. Calderon thought the man before
him looked fairly prosperous by Ibague standards.
At least his shoes were polished. He nodded.
"An academy. For soccer." He said and raised an
eyebrow at Juancar. "But you're too old."

Juancar burst out laughing. "I like you," he said.

Calderon fished around in his jacket pocket and came out with a bent business card and handed it to Juancar. "Yul Calderon," he said. "I am the manager."

Juancar looked at the card. "And evidently the head of marketing too," he quipped, nodding his head at the yellow posters Calderon had under his arm.

Calderon grinned. "The cost is ten thousand," he said. "Per month." He waited for the usual flinch whenever he told the price of his school, but Juancar did not blink an eye.

"Juan Carlos Restrepo," he said, shoving out his hand and Calderon shook it. "My friends call me Juancar."

"You have a boy? Juancar?" Calderon asked.

"Not just any boy," Juancar said. "The best lefty you have ever seen."

Calderon pretended not to care. Most parents always thought highly of their kids' talents. "Bring him to a try out. I am recruiting the U7 squad now," Calderon said.

"Perfect," Juancar said. "He plays two years

above his grade."

"Don't tell me he's five," Calderon said.

"Okay I won't," Juancar said. "We'll see you in the morning. I'm only in town for the weekend. I have got to get back to Bogota, where I work."

Calderon studied Juancar for a moment then nodded. "I'll give him a shot," he said.

"A very wise decision," Juancar said with a smile, then turned and headed up the street toward home.

Calderon watched him walk away, then remembered something. "Juancar!" He shouted after him.

Juancar turned back.

"What's his name?"

"James," Juancar shouted back. "James Rodriguez!"

Then he said goodbye and continued on his way home.

Calderon watched him go, then went over to the next telephone pole and stapled a yellow poster to it.

Chapter Nine

A WEEK LATER, James joined his teammates on the field behind the green and yellow store front announcing *Club Deportivo Academia Tolimense De Fútbol.*

He was skinny and frail compared to the rest. He was also the smallest boy on the squad. When he first started playing for Tolimense the staff pegged him for a brilliant left foot and nothing else. But within weeks they learned, it was the head on his shoulders that made him a star player. He may have looked frail and thin, but when that whistle blew, he was a shooting star. His intelligence and his ability to absorb everything he was taught by the coaches put him far out in front of the other players despite their size and age.

The Tolimense Academy actually had no field of its own. They practiced on a small patch of land in Ibague down the street from the Manuel

Murillo Toro Stadium where James and his mom and stepdad spent so many hours watching matches.

What they had was a bumpy lot with grass and weeds, clapboard fences all around, and boys learning and perfecting the art of the beautiful game.

For James, age meant nothing. Only skill counted on the field. He had only played with boys his own age once at Tolimense and was promoted almost immediately after a couple of friendlies where his skill put him way beyond anyone else on the younger squad.

In one of the games, the team was awarded a free kick. James ran and grabbed the ball. Another kid, Diego Norona, walked over to him. "I usually take the free kicks."

James liked Diego, but he felt he knew what he had to do. He wanted to make that kick.

Instead of saying anything, he put the ball on the ground and gave Norona a nod.

Norona grinned back. "You could at least say please," he said.

James got down on one knee and pantomimed begging.

Norona cracked up. "Okay," he said cheerfully. "I guess you must really want it, huh?"

James nodded without saying a word.

Norona thought about it. No one had ever taken the ball from him. Free kicks were his thing. But he liked the new kid and knew he was good. "Go for it," he said. "Get it over the wall. That's how we do it around here."

James looked at him, but did not nod.

He heard the whistle.

James kicked and the ball curled outside the wall of players and bent beautifully right past the keeper and into the goal.

The whole team cheered. Norona rushed him and hugged him. "That was unreal!" He held his hand up and James slapped him a high-five. James grinned broadly, but did not utter a word. He was afraid to talk and he had not ever said anything to anyone on the team yet.

He was afraid he'd stutter and they would make

fun of him, and that would be it.

So he just smiled. A big wide, beautiful smile.

That day, Diego Norona became his first friend.

Later that night, in their house in the Jordan neighborhood of Ibague, built atop a drugstore, James lay in bed, wide awake. A book was next to him on the nightstand. He knew what he was going to do. But first he needed to talk to his stepfather. "Papa?" He called out.

Juancar appeared in the doorway a few moments later. "Mm?" He asked. "Do you need something?"

James nodded and Juancar stepped over to his bed and sat down on the side of it. "What is it, son?"

"I had fun today," he said. "I scored a great goal," he said.

"I know," Juancar said. "I was there. So, maybe you like soccer after all?"

"Maybe," James said softly and blushed.

Juancar hugged him. "That's how it always is," he said. "Good night."

James smiled and Juancar left the room. When he was sure he was gone, James turned on the bedside lamp and snatched up his book. He had made up his mind. If he was going to have friends, then he was going to have to talk. He had a small light next to his bed and he opened his book of fairy tales.

Juancar and Pilar were in the kitchen, sharing a late night snack. It was a weekend where Juancar was down from his job in Bogota. When he realized that Pilar had to return home to Ibague, he promised he would come home at least every other weekend. Family was everything to him and James needed a father.

Pilar heard it first. It was a muffled voice, coming from the other side of the house. They listened carefully and realized the voice was coming from James' room. Juancar gave Pilar a curious look. They both got up and tiptoed across the house to James' bedroom doorway and peeked in.

James was in bed, reading.

Out loud.

He read the words, one by one, under the yellow chevron of light of his bedside lamp. His voice stammered and stopped and started in fits, but he never gave up and he kept reading one word to the next, one sentence at a time, getting a little better with each page turn.

Pilar had a tear in the corner of her eye. Juancar hugged her.

"He'll be great," he assured her.

"I know," she said in a muffled voice.

After a few weeks, Pilar and Juancar, whenever he was down from Bogota, became used to hearing the soft murmurs of their son's voice coming from his room at night. James also knew when to quit. When he couldn't keep his eyes open anymore, that's when he stopped. Then he reached down to the floor, picked up his blue and white ball, brought it into bed with him, and turned out the light.

Some nights all that talking made him hoarse, and some nights he fell asleep in the middle of a sentence. But he never gave up. His mom and stepdad always told him to keep doing the things that made him feel good and stop doing the things that didn't, and reading out loud made him feel good. And as the months flew by, he got pretty good at it. Juancar enrolled him with a speech therapist and very slowly, he improved.

Pilar, who was able to quit her job, thanks to

Juancar, sat in the stands every day James was on the field, training or playing a match. And when the team went on the road, she went along. They were inseparable.

Chapter Ten

THREE THINGS HAPPENED IN 1998 that changed James's life. First, his sister, Juana Valentina Restrepo Rubio was born on May 22, to his mother Pilar and his stepfather Juancar. Second, he watched every match of the 1998 World Cup where one of his heroes, Zinedine Zidane, was named Man of the Match. He was disappointed that another one of his heroes, Francesco Totti who played for Roma, was not called up for the Italians. He loved the way Totti played and copied him whenever he could.

The third thing was that he changed his mind about his future.

James and Diego walked out together to another practice when Diego asked James, "Do you want to be a pro when you grow up?" never expecting to get an answer. He knew he wouldn't get an answer because he asked him this question almost every time they took the field together.

He expected James to give him the usual answer: shake his head and say nothing. There was nothing special about the day, at least in Diego's mind. In fact, it was exactly the same kind of day as the day before: clear, foggy down below in the valley, and cold.

"Yes," James said.

Beto, another team mate, was already out on the field and he turned around. When he heard James utter that single word, he thought he was hearing things.

Diego froze and stopped what he was doing. "*What* did you say?!" He shouted at his friend.

James grinned back at him. "I s-said, yes!" Then he giggled.

"He talks!" Diego shouted.

All the boys stopped what they were doing when they heard what Diego said.

Coach Alvaro Guzman also looked surprised. In fact, no one on the field thought they had heard right. No one had actually heard James speak. They had played more than twenty matches and won most of them. They loved him and adored his talents. But his voice was a mystery.

"And he wants to play pro!" Diego announced proudly.

James, however, heard it all. He blushed and tried to continue practice as if nothing special had happened. Why was everyone making such a big deal just because he changed his mind. Then he realized it wasn't that he wanted to play pro, but by watching Zinedine Zidane play, he wanted to be like him when he grew up. The boys, on the other hand, were excited because he spoke for the first time.

Okay, so he never talked, but after all these months of practice he wanted to try out his voice. It was all very scientific, in his own mind. He loved science and he loved engineering just like his stepdad. His favorite books were about building stuff and engineering. It made sense to try out a little experiment with the team.

Guzman stepped up to James and put his face close to the boy's so no one else could hear. "Is this true?" He asked in a very low voice.

"Y-yessir," James said. The whole thing was starting to make him feel nervous.

Guzman grinned broadly but kept staring at him. "Excellent," he whispered. Juancar was there when practice was over and when they got in the car, he pulled something from out of a bag he kept next to him. "For you, son," Juancar said and handed him a number 10 Roma jersey with TOTTI on the back. "That was a great training, by the way."

James was so excited, he took off his team jersey and pulled on the new one and shoved his chest out proudly. Then his face grew serious. "Why wasn't Totti in the World Cup, papa Juancar?" He asked.

"Maybe his coach thought he wasn't ready. But one day he will play — and he'll win the World Cup.

"How?"

"There is a time for everything. If you are really great — your greatness will open up and blossom like a flower."

"So Totti is like a f-flower?" James asked.

His stepdad laughed a long laugh. "Yes, I guess so," he said with a broad grin.

James giggled and looked down at his new jersey.

He loved it.

The next day they were all on a bus to
Barranquilla on the Caribbean Sea side of Columbia.
The boys sat up front near the driver and the staff
and families sat in back. The whole Restrepo family
traveled when James traveled with the team.
They never missed an away match. This road trip,
however, was a big deal. The ride alone was ten
hours. Almost 500 kilometers.

None of the boys had ever seen the sea. Any sea.
Columbia was surrounded by them on either
side: the Pacific below the Central American chain
that ends in the Panama isthmus, connecting
North America to South America, Panama to
Columbia. And on the other side of the isthmus, the
Caribbean. And beyond that, the Atlantic.

It was all the boys talked about, the entire
journey. They had all seen rivers and lakes but
never so much water they could not see across.
"Are we t-there yet?" James joked with the driver
when they passed through Medellin. And again
when they motored through Monteria and again

through Cartagena. When they were finally close to Barranquilla, the driver announced their destination and the entire bus erupted in cheers and applause. Even the grown-ups cheered. The bus steered its way up a winding road to the top of a steep hill and when they crested it and could look down, they were looking at the Caribbean, so blue and broad that it filled all the windows. James stuck his head out the window and rested his chin on his arms and stared in wonder at the sea. It was chopped with white caps. Lightning-filled squalls dotted the horizon, flashing green when the sun dipped low.

Tolimense won their match, thanks to James. No one wanted to leave. The air near the sea helped everyone sleep more soundly and Pilar and Juancar loved it. But when the match was over, the bus turned around the next morning and headed back to Ibague.

The sun was still up when James and his family arrived home. And when they went inside, Juancar turned on the television and sat down on the sofa. There was a match on. Pilar went into the kitchen to feed baby Juana Valentina. Out in the street, a small parade of musicians passed by on their way to the Conservatory of Tolima, playing a familiar Columbian folk song. Pilar happily hummed along. Ibague was known as *The Musical City of Colombia.*

James stepped into the doorway and watched his mother. She felt his eyes on her and looked up. He was wearing his new number 10 jersey, beaming. "That is one nice jersey," she remarked.

"T-thanks," he replied and stood there for another moment.

Pilar sensed he something else to say. "Was there something else, son?"

James stayed silent for another moment, then blurted it out perfectly. "I've decided — I want to be a professional when I grow up!"

Pilar thought about it for a moment. Her eyes welled-up with tears and she did not care if James noticed.

"Did I m-make you sad?" He asked.

"No, mijo," she cooed. "You make me happy. The way you speak. You work so hard, every night, reading. I'm so proud of you."

"I p-practice and get better," he said.

Juancar appeared behind him in the doorway. "Match is starting, son," he said. James looked up at him and he draped his arm over his shoulders and guided him back to the living room to watch the game.

Chapter Eleven

JAMES DID NOT THINK he needed the speech therapist anymore. "Why?" He asked. "I-I don't need him. I'm doing okay by myself," he told his stepfather.

"Trust me, I'm your father," Juancar replied.

James glared at Juancar. "Y-you're not my father!" He shouted at him.

The room grew perfectly quiet. James could not believe he said that and wished he could stuff the cruel words back in his mouth.

Juancar was stung, but his love for the boy was stronger than a few mean words. He did not give up. "I'm not? Then who was there for you all these years?" He asked. "Who bandaged your knees when you fell in the street and who picked you up when you could not stand? Who carried you when you could not walk and who still comes to you in the night when you have a nightmare? Who raised you?"

The words came at James like a hurricane and he could not control himself any longer. He burst out crying. "I'm sorry, papa Juancar, I-I'm s-so sorry — I didn't mean it," he sobbed and fell into Juancar's arms and snuggled up against the man. "You-are-my-father," he said.

"Then let me help you," Juancar whispered.

James looked up at his father and nodded.

A week later they sat side by side in in the speech specialist's waiting room. There was no one else in the room but James was still terrified. He could take the field against a team of boys twice his size and not feel any fear, so why was he so afraid? He wanted to get better, didn't he?

When the speech therapy session was finished, the doctor gave James some homework. "I like the idea of you reading out loud to yourself," he said. "Keep doing what you are doing. You have a soft voice, a warm smile, and from what I hear a great left foot!

"Will I g-get better?" James asked weeks later.

"You already are," the speech therapist said.

"I am?"

"Look. I've gotten to know you well over the past month. You are not only talented in soccer — but in all things. Including speaking."

James was embarrassed at the praise, but it turned out the words the speech therapist spoke were true. Because of his spectacular soccer talent, James had moved up to an older squad at Tolimense over the years he had been there.

And when the team participated in the Pony Futbol Cup in Medellin, young James was a key player in their success.

The whole family was there for the tournament.

In the first match, Tolimense versus Medellin, they were down 2-1 against Medellin and if they lost they would be out of the tournament.

Coach Guzman took James aside with ten minutes left in the match. "You're the reason we're here," he told him. "You can do it."

He gave his coach a wink and charged out on the field. Within seconds, he got the ball and was surrounded by two defenders. He was fouled and Tolimense was awarded a free kick. And he was about to take it.

He knew he needed to surprise the other team. He knew they expected him to go over the wall.

He heard the whistle.

He kicked with his left, bent the ball around the left side of the wall and into the net.

The goal keeper just stared at the ball and did not move.

There was a second of silence. It was as if no one comprehended what had just happened.

GOAL!

The crowd of over 2000 were on their feet. Medellin was never able to score again, the match ended in a draw, and Tolimense would be back to fight another day.

Gustavo Upegui Lopez, also known as Don Gustavo, recently purchased the Medellin second division youth soccer team, Envigado FC. He was a man who loved the beautiful game more than anything else.

He already heard about the 12-year-old boy, living in Ibague, the one with a magical left foot. He had to see for himself. And he did not have to go very far.

Don Gustavo caught up with Alfaro Guzman at the opening of the team tunnel. They exchanged handshakes.

"Señor Guzman! Your forward — James Rodriguez — is a genius," he said.

"He is a hard worker. We have helped him expand his game," Guzman said.

"You have done an excellent job," Don Gustavo gushed. "And it has not gone unnoticed."

Guzman knew the man and he knew how wealthy and powerful he was. He waited to hear what Don Gustavo had to say.

"We want him," Don Gustavo said. "For Independiente Medellin."

Guzman's smile faded.

Don Gustavo studied the coach. "Name your price," he said.

"He's not for sale," Guzman coldly shot back, then turned and walked off down the tunnel.

Don Gustavo watched him go for a moment. "Not yet, he isn't," he muttered to himself.

Near the end of the tournament, the television cameras showed up. So did more than 5000 fans. The *Estadio Atanasio Girardot* where the tournament took place, had never seen these kinds of crowds for a youth tournament in its history. Word got out about a new Pibe and hordes of fans showed up.

James was impressed by the crowd. He had been touring the country with his squad and winning regularly. Kids started talking. Adults started talking. Fans started talking. All about the boy whose name was James, the one who played like magic.

He was instantly famous. And that made him nervous.

James emerged from the locker rooms onto the pitch and the crowd erupted when they saw him. He stopped in shock, unsure of what was happening in the stands. He turned and saw his parents sitting in the first row so he trotted over to them. "Who is here?" He asked. "Who are they cheering?"

Juancar burst out laughing. "They are cheering for you!" He said. "Thirteen goals in 9 games?! Get out there and give them something to cheer about!"

James nodded, then took a deep breath, and took the field.

Everyone was on their feet, cheering him, shouting in unison, "JAMES! JAMES!" The Colombian way: *Ha-mez Ha-mez Ha-mez…*

They knew his name. How could they be cheering him? He was just a thirteen-year-old kid!

His heart raced. It was exciting. But he knew he had to get his head in the game.

Don Gustavo got out of his car in front of the stadium and flanked by two men from Envigado FC, marched through the gates. He was here for only one reason. And it wasn't to plead with Alfaro Guzman.

Chapter Twelve

JAMES RACED DOWN THE FIELD, dribbling the ball but he was tackled and he could not develop his attack. It angered him. Frustrated him.

Juancar was on his feet, shouting instructions from the first row.

James heard him and stopped and glared at him. The opposing midfielders stole the ball. Furious, James stomped off the field in anger.

Coach Calderon saw what happened and pointed an angry finger at Juancar. "Let him be! I'm the coach!"

When James reached the sideline, Calderon caught him and stopped him. "What are you doing?"

"I-I'm out," James said and tried to twist past his coach.

"You're out when I say you're out," Calderon said and pushed him back onto the field. "Don't listen to the crowd, even if it is your own father.

You are your own player. Now get out there!"

James clenched and unclenched his fists to cool down, then caught his breath and nodded. One more second, then he charged back onto the field.

Calderon turned his back on the field and closed his eyes in relief.

Diego had the ball. James raised his hand and Diego kicked a half volley, praying he could hit his team mate like they had planned. James controlled the ball in his chest and down to his feet — twisted around, and fired off a shot. The ball hurtled like a guided missile and hit the right side of the net.

It was the same move he did on the streets of Ibague when he was a little kid.

But much better.

Calderon almost tripped over his own feet, he was so surprised. He raised his arms in the air and hopped as high as he could, screaming. "GOOAAALLL!!"

The whistle blew.

The match was over. Academia Tolimense won the Pony Futbol Tournament, 2–1.

Don Gustavo was on his feet, watching the field as James was instantly surrounded by his team mates.

A television camera was shoved in the boy's face and a reporter stuck a microphone at him and started firing off questions. James was polite and answered every question he was asked.

Don Gustavo turned to his companions from Envigado. "I have to have him," he said.

"I'll get his coach," one of the men said.

"No," Don Gustavo said. "Find his parents. I'll speak to his coach." Although he was dressed casually, for a match, his men wore suits and looked like the Men in Black. They rushed off immediately. He was still trying to process what he had just seen. He had the kid's stats and witnessed for himself the boy's ability to mastermind a play in the earlier game. The boy was quickly getting attention for people in the know.

He was obviously great. This boy had super peripheral vision and great skills. He returned his attention to the field and saw Guzman talking with Calderon.

He made his way to the coach. Calderon knew what he was about to say.

Don Gustavo spoke first. "I'm developing a squad at Envigado that we plan on taking pro," he told him.

Calderon wasn't going to give up without a fight. "The boy is too valuable to me and I still have a couple years with him. Let's talk when he's fourteen."

Don Gustavo smiled. "When he is fourteen, we expect he will be in our First Division."

Calderon knew he could not protest. It would always be what was best for James.

Don Gustavo patted Calderon's cheek. "Don't worry Yul. We will take care of you and your academy, you have my word," he said.

Calderon knew he was lying and he wouldn't pay, but that was beside the point. What was best for the boy? "Do I have a choice, Don Gustavo?" He asked.

Don Gustavo shot him a final, cruel smile. "No."

A few minutes later, Juancar and Pilar had a

conversation with Don Gustavo. Juancar knew of him. Everyone in Medellin did. Some called him the Mayor of Medellin. Juancar had expected this to happen, he knew how talented his stepson was and had prepared himself and Pilar for the rush of teams who would want him, especially after winning the Pony Futbol Tournament. He also knew Don Gustavo owned Envigado. "So you would train him at Independiente Medellin? Not Envigado?" Juancar asked. He remained calm even though he was exploding inside. There was no way this was going to be a bad deal and his stepson deserved the best.

"We want to groom him for Envigado and the professionals. We believe the best place to train him will be as a member of Independiente," Don Gustavo said.

"Of course you know, we live in Ibague," Pilar said.

"We will move you to Medellin," Don Gustavo said without missing a beat. "A nice apartment next to *El Dorado,* everything will be taken care of." *El Dorado* was the name of the field where Independiente Medellin and Envigado practiced.

"This is much too far for me to commute, to Bogota and back," Juancar, explained.

Don Gustavo smiled. "We expect you to quit your job in Bogota. We are very serious about James' career. We believe he will go all the way and he will need his parents to always be a part of his life. Family is everything to us. We will provide you with jobs in Medellin; you have nothing to worry about. Ever again." He smiled. "We want you to think of us as family."

He reached out his hand and after a moment, Juancar shook it. So did Pilar.

Guzman watched Juancar then Pilar shake Don Gustavo's hand and knew he had lost his star player forever.

James David Rodriguez Rubio, just 13 years old and already a well-known midfielder on the Columbian youth circuit, was moving from his soccer home at *Academia Tolimense* to *Independiente Medellin.*

Chapter Thirteen

JAMES' FAMILY PULLED UP ROOTS IN IBAGUE in
2004 and moved to a new apartment in Medellin,
across the street from *El Dorado,* the field where
Independiente Medellin and all the other Envigado
squads trained: James, his parents and his sister and
his dog, Simon.

The Envigado Futbol Club called itself the *The
Quarry of Heroes.* The Envigado suburb used to
be once one of the most violent areas in Columbia.
With the change in the Columbian constitution, it
had quickly evolved into a true cultural destination
and the epicenter of Columbia's rebirth in soccer.

On the day the family moved in, of all the
appliances the family owned, the first thing Juancar
plugged in was the television set. The couch had
still not been brought in from the moving truck,
so James and his stepfather sat on the floor in front
of the set. A match was on between Manchester

United and Arsenal. And James got his first look
at the newest player on the Red Devils, a good
looking boy from Madeira, an island off the coast
of Portugal. He was wearing David Beckham's
old jersey, number seven. His name was Cristiano
Ronaldo dos Santos Aveiro, but the television
announcers referred to him as Ronaldo.

James thought he was brilliant and kept his eyes
glued to the set every time the Red Devils got the
ball because it eventually wound up at Ronaldo's
feet. He was better than anyone he had ever seen
and James did not bother putting up his old posters
of soccer legends on his bedroom wall. He reserved
the space for his new hero, Cristiano Ronaldo.

The next day, James took the field for a friendly
with the older Envigado squad. Juancar, Pilar, and
Juana Valentina were there for the practice game.
James stole the ball and when he turned to race
downfield, he was tackled by the tallest player
on the other side. James flew through the air and
landed on his back, knocking the wind out of him.

Pilar gasped and leaped to her feet.

James moaned and looked up as his teammate

reached out a hand and helped him up.

The boy needs to get stronger, Juancar thought.

A few days later, James took the field and while he waited for training to begin, he practiced the move he saw Ronaldo make on TV. He rolled the ball inside with his left foot, then crossed over the ball with his right foot, stopping it with his left. All he had to do was drag the ball back to the other side with his left and take control. Except he stepped on the top of the ball instead and fell flat on his face!

His teammates laughed so hard they almost fell over themselves.

Hernandez, the fitness coach sat in the stands with Juancar, watching James and when he fell in the dirt, he closed his eyes and wondered what he was going to do with this gawky kid.

"He is too frail," someone said and both men looked around to see the source of the voice. "But not for long."

Omar "El Misio" Suarez walked down the row of seats and sat down next to them.

Suarez winked at Juancar. "Thank you for calling

me, Juancar," he whispered and shook Juancar's hand.

"Misio!" Hernandez said, recognizing him. "What is the most renowned private coach in Medellin doing at El Dorado?"

Suarez grinned and jerked his head toward Juancar. "A little birdy told me you needed a miracle," he said.

Hernandez grinned at Juancar. "You really know how to pull things together for your son, don't you?" He asked.

Juancar shrugged. "He wants to wear the yellow and black. His dream is to play midfielder for *Los Cafeteros*," he said, referring to the Colombian national team. "Besides, he's the only son I got."

The men chuckled.

Hernandez put his hand on Suarez's shoulder and pointed to James out on the field. "That's him," he said.

"I'm way ahead of you. I've seen him. At the Pony Futbol tournament. How could I not? Thirteen goals in nine games? Isn't that a record?" Suarez asked.

"I'm afraid he's going to get hurt," Hernandez said.

"I know you are," Suarez said, "We can take care of that. However, I watched him play in the tournament and our boy has another problem."

"What is that?" Juancar asked.

"His left foot. He's too dependent on it."

James could see them from where he stood on the field. He had eyes like a hawk and may have had a hard time talking, but he could read lips. Juancar, that man and Senor Hernandez were talking about *him.* Juancar waved him over.

He dropped his ball and dribbled it all the way over to the stands with his right foot.

Suarez watched James come across the field towards them, grinning the whole way. "You don't suppose he heard what we were saying, do you? About his left foot?" He asked and they all looked at each other. Juancar blushed.

"I uh — may have mentioned to him to uh — favor his right foot today," Juancar confessed. "In case you didn't know, he's very good with both."

All three men laughed and Suarez laughed the loudest.

"D-did you w-want to see me, sir?" James asked stopping in front of the stands, picking up the ball.

Suarez leaned forward in his seat. "I am Senor Suarez," he said. "Your new trainer. I just wanted to let you know I am looking forward to working with you."

James shoved out his hand and Suarez shook it. "Thank you, sir. M-me too."

"Call me Misio," Suarez said and gave the boy a wink.

"Thank you, Mister Misio," James said.

Chapter Fourteen

JAMES WAS NOT ONLY A REAL LIVE TEENAGE SOCCER PRODIGY, he was also an animated character on a TV screen. The real James made the avatar of himself in the PlayStation FIFA character creator. The real James flicked the controller and turned his 3D animated midfield avatar around on the TV screen just as another animated midfielder on his 3D animated squad shot the ball to him. With his back to the goal, he caught the ball in his chest, let it drop, twisted his body and flicked the ball into the net, completely fooling the goalkeeper.

He jumped up from the couch and let the PlayStation controller drop as he raised both hands high into the air and shouted, "YESSSSSS!" terrifying Simon the dog, who scrambled away from him in terror, his claws click-clacking on the floor as he raced away safely to his favorite place behind the chair.

"Sorry, Simon!" James said.

Pilar stood in the doorway, watching and chuckling. "I saw that," she said.

"I'm sorry, I-I think I scared Simon," he quickly shot back.

"I'm not talking about the dog, James," she said. "I'm talking about the goal. The goal you did on your PlayStation! I've seen you do it before. For real."

"I-I'm practicing f-for the World Cup!" He said and gave her two thumbs up.

Pilar laughed. "From your mouth to God's ear!"

James grinned. "W-well we have had m-many blessings so far!"

She crossed her arms and saw the piles of clothes on the couch and recognized them as his uniforms. "Aren't you forgetting something?" She asked, indicating the piles of clean but unfolded uniforms.

"Oh!" He said. "Right!"

"I'll get it," she said and hurried into the kitchen and returned moments later with an ironing board and an iron, handing both to him. He took them and opened the board and plugged in the iron and waited, flipping the PlayStation to regular TV. He licked his fingertip and touched the iron and when it was hot enough, began ironing his uniforms. Shorts first, then shirt, then shorts, then…

There was a knock at the door and he started for the door and she stopped him. "You keep ironing, I'll get it," she said. He threw the door open and Don Gustavo was standing there. "Mr. Lopez!" She said, surprised to see him. "Please come in, what can we do for you?"

Don Gustavo stepped into the house. He seemed hesitant to her. "Can we talk?"

"Of course," she said.

Then he saw James ironing his uniforms. "So, this is why you are always so neat when you show up for games. You being punished for something?"

James laughed and shook his head. "P-part of my training, at Tolimense," he said.

"Ironing clothes? How does that help your penalty kick?" Don Gustavo asked.

"Presentation," Pilar answered. "It is as important as discipline."

The guest looked flabbergasted. He glanced over

at Pilar. "I'm surprised."

"You shouldn't be. It wasn't just James' talent in soccer that brought you to him."

Don Gustavo smiled. "No. It was how he handled himself. On and off the field. The problem is," he said, "He is too frail. We would like to invest a lot of money in him but I'm afraid he will be injured the first time he takes the field as an Envigado." He glanced over at James, then back to Pilar. "Let's take a walk."

He led the way and he and Pilar walked side-by-side. "Can I be honest with you?"

Pilar nodded.

"They haven't said it in so many words but, the front office has basically given up on him."

"Oh no!" Pilar said and bit her lip.

He stopped and faced her. "What is important is not that they give up on him, but that you don't give up on me. What do they know? They never won anything until James showed up. I bought them out. His rights belong to me. And I'm moving him straight to Envigado."

"Does Juancar know about this?"

"Of course. It was his idea. He asked for Omar Suarez to come in and train him and I agreed."

"I've heard of him," she said.

"Of course you have. For private instructors — he is as good as it gets. I just need one thing from you. That's why I came here personally."

"Name it," she replied.

"We want to put James on a hormone treatment program. I need your permission."

Pilar looked at him. "Is it going to hurt him?"

"We would never do anything to harm James," he said. "You would never forgive me, and neither would our country."

"Our country?"

"Columbia," he replied. "We see him going all the way."

Pilar took Don Gustavo's hand. "Thank you. For helping my son."

"He's like a son to me too," he said. "More than that, he's a very lucky kid. He's got a lot of fathers pulling for him."

Pilar smiled. "He does indeed."

James started on the hormone treatments and gradually felt himself grow stronger, week by week, month by month, and match by match. In January of 2006, when he was just fourteen, Don Gustavo was ready to let him make his debut as a professional.

When the big day arrived, James stood in the locker room. Don Gustavo came in with an orange and white jersey slung over his shoulder and stopped in front of him. James had grown almost as tall as the man who brought him to Envigado. Don Gustavo was proud of his prodigy. Then he tossed him the jersey.

"Number ten," he said. "You earned it."

James held back the tears as he threw on the number 10 jersey. It was a great honor to wear it and it was especially sweet getting it from the one man outside of his own family that always believed in him.

When James was walking off the field after the game, Don Gustavo walked with him. "I want you to promise me something," he said.

"Okay," James said.

"No matter what happens to me, keep going. Your father and I believe in you and I think you can be the biggest star our country has seen since Valderrama."

"What might happen to you?" James asked.

Don Gustavo riveted him with a stare. "Just promise me."

"Okay," James said. "I promise."

He gave the boy a hug. "Thank you. Now get in there and change, we're all going out to celebrate. We're having a great dinner. Your family, and mine."

A month later, Don Gustavo Upegui Lopez was dead.

Chapter Fifteen

JAMES SAT ON THE SIDELINES at *El Dorado,* his head in his hands, tears streaming down his face. It had been like this all week. Occasionally, he looked up to watch his team practice but his head was definitely not in the game. He loved his family. And next to them, he loved Don Gustavo, who was like a father to him. And now he was gone forever. He remembered the talk they had just the other week. He wondered if his mentor knew he would be shot to death in his own home by his enemies.

It terrified James and he stopped speaking when he heard the news. That was over a week ago. His mother and father brought him to practice every day, but he would not take the field. "When you are ready, then get back out there," Juancar had said to him.

"We can't keep doing this, Jamesito," Hugo Brown said, walking over to him. "I need you."

Brown was the head coach of Envigado and instrumental in helping Don Gustavo keep James on his training regimen when the rest of the front office had given up on him, due to his small stature. Hugo was a big burly man with short black hair that was starting to gray.

James looked up at his coach, but he would not talk.

Hugo could see he had been crying. He stood over him. "Do you think, for one second, that Don Gustavo would approve of what you are doing here?"

James was afraid to look him in the eye. His heart was just in so much pain, he could not move. He felt paralyzed.

"I know you are in pain. But Don Gustavo wanted you to play. This is your responsibility. Your destiny," the coach said, turning, blowing his whistle and joining the squad out on the field, leaving James behind.

James knew Mr. Brown was right. Don Gustavo himself told him to never give up. He could not do it now. He had to grit his teeth and face his fears.

He took a deep breath, then trotted out on the field to join his new squad. Hugo Brown saw him coming first and turned to watch. Then the rest of the team saw him and they all turned around to watch him run toward them, and when he got there, they surrounded him and hugged him and welcomed him back.

That night, just before Juancar and Pilar drifted off to sleep, they heard their son reading aloud. It lasted late into the night and for Pilar, it was soothing. Her son's voice was clear, and his stammer was gone. James read every night, from March until May, not only because he was anxious to improve his speech so he could do better with his studies in school, but because he was nervous. Whatever it was inside him that kept the words from coming out, he wanted vanquished. He wanted it gone. Forever. He knew what was coming for him in May. Hugo Brown told him he would be starting for the First Division of Envigado, and in his debut, he would be facing Cucuta Deportivo, his hometown team, and the team his biological father played for so many years before.

Hugo Brown delivered the message himself. "I spoke with your father and he's coming to the match to see you play," he said.

"They always come, him and mama. They come to every game," James said.

"I'm not talking about Juancar, James," Hugo Brown said. "I'm talking about Wilson James Rodriguez Bedoya, your birth father."

"But — why?" James asked with astonishment.

"He says he wants to support his team, his beloved Cucuta Deportivo," Brown said. "But I know better." He pursed his lips and took a breath before continuing. "He wants to see you."

James had a hard time looking at Coach Brown. He wished he had never had this conversation. "Well, I don't want to see him."

"No one's saying you have to forgive him, I wouldn't put that on anybody, especially a kid like you."

"I'm no kid," James said and wished he hadn't.

Hugo Brown studied the boy and smiled. "Hey. You have a family. What are you worried about?"

"I'm not," James said.

Brown could hardly hear him. "Okay. Remember this. We have your back. All you have to do is go out there and win," he said. "But I don't want to put any pressure on you."

"You already did, coach," he said.

James stood in the changing room clutching a scuffed-up ball to his orange and whites, the team colors of Envigado FC. Even the ball was striped in orange.

"Is that your new girlfriend, James?" Fredy Guarin shouted from across the room and all the boys on the team laughed. He had made some friends coming up from Independiente Medellin, including Guarin, Giovanni Moreno and Dorlan Pabon, all terrific players in their own right. And they were all there that day in May.

"It relaxes me," James said and shot them a calm smile. His nerves always went all jangly for the five minutes just before the start of a match. And holding a game ball close to his chest always calmed him down. His nerves today were especially rattled. It was the first time playing with these guys.

The fact that his real father was probably out there in the stands, was something he could shut out. Juancar taught him how to focus and his ability to shut out the things that might distract him from doing what he wanted to do most, win, he owed to the man who raised him.

James took the field at El Dorado on May 21 and knew exactly who he was and where he was. He was 14 years, 10 months, and 8 days old. It was hot that day in Envigado. And somewhere in the stands, the man who abandoned him and his mother all those years ago, was watching. His head was talking again and he shook the lousy thought away. He had a match to win.

Chapter Sixteen

THE LOCAL PAPER IN ENVIGADO started calling James the crack, which meant, *the best of the best,* and it was too distracting and tempting to believe. Juancar had taught him to be grateful for the praise, but to ignore it, even if he believed it was true. It began when he was twelve when he played for Tolimense in Pony Futbol and was surrounded by reporters. He shook them off then and nothing has changed over the past two years except he was a better player.

He shook all those thoughts away as anxiety left him and he got his head into the game.

The hormone treatments that Don Gustavo had ordered were obviously working, but not quick enough. He had grown some inches on the hormone treatments, but he was still skinny and that made him a target for the Cucuta players.

His eyes scanned the stands where he knew his

father must be sitting. Would he recognize him? Just the thought made him hesitate and he felt like if he needed to talk to his father, the words would not come out when he needed them. His mother, sister, and Juancar were in the stands, down in front, and seeing them there, just as they always had done, day in and day out. relaxed him. His nervousness left him as soon as his feet touched the grass.

Coach Brown told James, "Do what you know, kid."

James nodded and took his position, the whistle blew, and they were off.

Thirty minutes later there was still no score and when the ball sailed to James, he caught it in his chest. The Cucuta defender was on him. He hit the ball with the inside of his right foot and tunneled it through the defender's legs in a perfect nutmeg, raced around him and was ready to smash it into the goal, but the opponent was furious and shouldered him to the grass, then took one last derisive look at the boy he had just floored, before moving on.

Pain shot up James's leg. He gritted his teeth and waited for the pain to subside. The crowd leaped to their feet, booing.

The ref flashed a yellow card at the other player.

James tasted the grass and in that instant, looked across the pitch to the stands and saw him. Midfield. About five rows back. To the left of his family. He recognized him instantly from the picture his mother had given him, even though he barely had any memory of him. His hair was grey and he wore a Tolimense jersey. At least it wasn't one from Cucuta, James thought.

The ref stood over him. "Can you get up?" He asked.

James nodded and wordlessly got to his feet.

The crowd cheered. He did not look to see if his father was cheering.

James got ready to take the free kick. The Cucuta squad formed a wall.

James lined himself up and took the shot with his right and kicked hard.

The ball curled over the edge of the wall and bent into the goal just as the goalkeeper spread his hands helplessly to stop it.

The ball sailed peacefully into the net behind him and the crowd leaped to their feet, cheering wildly.

James only watched one person in the crowd. His father. He was on his feet, cheering. He stared at him and then something amazing happened. His father saw him watching him and held up his hand and gave him the peace sign. James felt his heart race. He slowly raised his hand up and gave him the same signal back, and even at this distance, he saw the smile spread across his father's face.

"Wow," James said to himself.

Then he was surrounded by his team mates as they hugged him and dove on him and when he finally extracted himself from the pile and returned his gaze to the stands, his father was gone.

They lost the game, but everyone in the stands knew they had just witnessed a star in the making.

Hugo Brown, his coach, wondered how he could keep James for at least a little while longer. Of course, he felt, if he had to lose him to a bigger team, he would help him get there.

James stayed loyal to Envigado and the following season he was moved up to the U17 squad and they were runners up in the South American Championships. In all, he scored nine more goals for his team. His family was there for every match and Juancar sent out DVDs of James' talents to a number of agents around the world.

In the 2008 season, James took the field for his first match. It would be the only match he played in 2008 for Envigado. In the stands were scouts from Boca Juniors, Lanus, and Birmingham City. And his new agent. Silvio Sandri.

He felt happy, and it wasn't long and the crowd was on their feet again when he scored another goal.

That is when he saw her for the first time. She was tall, with long dark hair. She was with a girl he knew from town, but in that moment, she was alone in the stands and to James, the way the lights were on behind her, it looked like she had a halo over her head. She was watching him and their eyes met. She shyly looked away when James was slammed by his team mates and brought to the ground. He got to his feet and led the boys in a quick dance, something they always did whenever they scored.

The two girls in the stands laughed. They waved him over.

James could not resist. When the game was over, he quickly left his team mates and raced to the stands. The girl he knew was already standing. "James, this is Daniela," she said.

James' heart raced. He never felt anything like this before in his life. He reached out his hand and she stretched her hand over the railing and touched the back of his hand.

She quickly took a pen from her purse and wrote something on a small piece of paper, folded it up and reached back over the rail and passed it to him.

"Nice to meet you, James," Daniela said.

Later, in the changing room, James pulled the piece of paper from his pocket and unfolded it. It had *Daniela Ospina* written in blue ink along with a telephone number.

James called her that night and they spoke until

her mother, Lucia, made them hang up. She told him that her brother David is a goal keeper, but he already knew that.

It was about that time of blooming romance and bidding wars for James' talents that The Argentinian team Banfield outbid the competition. The DVD his stepfather had sent out caught the attention of sports agent Silvio Sandri, and with James' and Juancar's agreement, Pilar signed the papers that would send her sixteen-year-old son to Buenos Aires alone and pay him more than $400,000. They chose Banfield because he was promised a fast track to their first team.

The Banfield management believed that James was a natural number ten. So he was told.

He was just 16 years old. His family had more money than they had ever seen in any of their lifetimes. And he was moving to Argentina. Alone.

Chapter Seventeen

BANFIELD WAS LOCATED on the outskirts of Buenos Aires, the capital of Argentina, and when James arrived there, it was freezing cold. Where the weather in Medellin was tropical, Buenos Aires was like an ice box. And if James thought the weather was frigid, he was not prepared for the cold reception he got from the managers and coaches of Banfield.

Jorge Burruchaga studied the boys as he walked across the grass to where they were lined-up. He was once an attacking midfielder for *Club Atletico Independiente* and later wound up managing that team for more than a year before coming over to manage Banfield. His reserve coach, Raul Wensel, stood next to him.

James felt awkward. He did not know a soul. This was his first day at the team in a foreign country. He was all alone, and already missing his family. Banfield had spent a lot of money on him and he wanted to make sure he did everything right.

That did not seem to mean anything to the men who managed and coached the team. Burruchaga and Wensel stopped in front of him. For some reason neither looked happy. Wensel wouldn't even look at him and that made him feel queasy.

Burruchaga finally spoke. "I want to welcome the little Colombian to Banfield," he announced, drilling James with a look and saying the word *Colombian* as if it were one of the words he was not allowed to say.

The name stung. Why didn't he call him by his name?

Wensel remained silent.

"Do you call everyone by their country name?" He asked.

Burruchaga just grinned. "Sorry. We don't get many outsiders, meaning anyone not born in Argentina. No offense. Silvio says you were a star on the first team in Envigado. Is that right?"

James reluctantly nodded.

"He said you were a crack," Burruchaga added. "Are you-?"

James felt embarrassed and could not find the words. "No, n-not really…"

"You are right. We make cracks here; we don't buy them. You start at the bottom. Is that understood, James?"

It was clear from the start that they had to find a place for the outsider they probably did not want. James did not expect to be placed on the first squad right away, but he did expect to play, considering how much Banfield had spent on him. But the freezing welcome he got was humiliating.

As the days went by, James played on the second, third and even the fourth team. But he did not get a shot at the first team. No one seemed impressed by him. No one cared. Months passed.

James made two phone calls every night. One to his family, and the other to Daniela. Then every night, feeling the frustration of loneliness, he wanted to cry. He hated it here. He wanted to go home.

The bus ride back to his small apartment in the lake city of Palermo, Buenos Aires, took an hour in good traffic.

James was looking forward to tonight. His mother would be calling. And he could speak to Juancar too and Juana Valentina. He missed them all desperately. His mother made a rule that they would call every other night.

He lived in a small apartment overlooking the river delta that separated Argentina and Uruguay. In fact, he could see Uruguay from his apartment window if he used binoculars. Most of the boys on the Banfield squads stayed at the pension lodge in Banfield, near the team headquarters, but not as nice. Juancar and Pilar found this place for him. He liked being near the water. It relaxed him.

When he got home he hurried to the window and looked out at the river. He checked the clock on his end table and walked to the telephone and sat staring at it for five minutes until it rang. He snatched it up and listened. It was his mother and he told her he was still miserable and lonely and that Burruchaga was still as mean as ever.

"I wish I would have gone with Fredy to Boca," he said. He was talking about his Envigado team mate Fredy Guarin who signed with the Boca Juniors. "At least I wouldn't be alone."

"Jamesito!" His mother scolded. "You're not alone. I'm right here."

"No, you are right there. I am right here." He said.

"I'm sorry, is that not enough?" She asked.

James hesitated. "I-I met someone. In Medellin. At a game. I talk to her after I talk to you."

"A girl?" His mother sounded suddenly on guard.

"Her name is Daniela. Her brother is David Ospina."

"The keeper?"

"Yes," James replied.

"This is great," she said. "Maybe she will cheer you up."

James knew he had her.

"Thank you, mama."

She passed the phone to his stepfather.

"Are you doing your studies at night?" Juancar asked.

"Yes sir," James said.

"Good. Don't forget who you are. You are my son. I have a reputation to uphold as an intellectual."

James chuckled. "Yes, papa, I am studying. I enjoy studying computer engineering just like you enjoy it — especially after a hard day of being abused and disrespected by the coaches."

Juancar burst out laughing. "You win. You are officially funnier than I. That was a pretty good speech by the way, I'm proud of you."

"No comment," James said and flashed a grin.

"Well, I have one," Juancar replied. "GO TO BED!"

James laughed and said his good-byes and hung up the phone. He immediately called Daniela.

"I wish you could come down to Buenos Aires," he pleaded.

"I want to, but my mother says 'no'", she replied.

It was the same every night. James's heart sunk.

Later that night, he opened a book on computer engineering, one that Juancar sent him, and read aloud for an hour. If anyone living in his building happened to be listening at his door, they would have thought he was a student of science and missed the fact that they were actually living next door to a soccer star in the making.

Chapter Eighteen

ANOTHER PRACTICE DAY. Burruchaga blew the whistle, ending a scrimmage.

The boys walked off the field toward the locker rooms. James was down. He had spoken to Daniela by phone last night and pleaded with her again to come join him in Argentina, but again, her mother would not allow it.

That is when he saw the man walking out of the tunnel and into the bright sunlight.

He recognized him immediately. It was Jairo Patiño. He had been on the Colombian national team that went to the semifinal of the *Confederations Cup* in 2003 and in 2005 to the *Concacaf Gold Cup* where they lost to Panama. Jairo was a midfielder from Atlético Nacional in Medellin where he played with Daniela's brother David Ospina. Before that, River Plate and before that, Newell's Old Boys.

He could not believe he was here in Banfield.

And, he was wearing Banfield colors.

James watched Jairo greet the staff, then immediately trot straight to him! James looked behind him to see where Jairo was going, thinking he was coming out on the field to speak to someone else, but no one was behind him. He turned back as Jairo stopped in front of him and stuck out his hand. "Jairo Patiño," he said. "I've been wanting to meet you for a long time, James."

Jairo was the same height and almost twice his age. When James grew up, he was already a star. James stared dumbly for a split second. The words. The words in his head. Were they lined up right? Why would Jairo Patiño look forward to meeting *him?!*

He shoved out his hand and grasped his fellow footballer's hand and shook it. The grip was firm and friendly. "Thank you, I-I know who you are, I am a big fan."

Jairo grinned, then put his hand on his heart and bowed slightly. "I am happy to play with you." Jairo started on the first team and James was still on the second but it was a nice gesture. James felt for the first time that he wasn't alone.

And then one day everything changed. The coach entered the locker room and handed him the number 10 jersey. "This is for you," he said. The jersey had *JAMES* emblazoned on the back.

James looked at the jersey in disbelief. "This is — a first team jersey," he said.

"That's right," Burruchaga said. "I'm glad your eyes still work."

James turned to the team and everyone cheered.

"Congratulations," Burruchaga said. "You worked hard and you deserve it."

After practice, in the locker room, the goal-keeper, Luchetti, tackled James, held him down, and shaved the hair from the middle of his head, all the way down to the scalp. James looked like someone had taken a lawnmower and cut a wide path down the middle of his head. He was mortified. In celebration, the rest of the team shaved the hair on their heads in insanely ridiculous patterns.

James Rodriguez was officially initiated into the First Team at Banfield.

The following week, Burruchaga was fired.

Chapter Nineteen

ONE DAY AFTER PRACTICE, James was about to take the bus home to his Palermo neighborhood apartment. He realized he did not have enough bus money to get home. The guys were all changing and getting ready to go back to their apartments or the pension and James wandered among them. "I need to borrow some change for bus fare," he pleaded. "Can you spare a few coins each? I should be able to scrape up enough to get home. If you do this for me, I will remember you in my speech when I win the Puskas Award!"

The boys all laughed.

"You know there's a coin shortage here, Coffee," Jairo said, using the nickname the team adopted for James, thanks to their ex-coach Burruchaga. "I'll run you home."

"Thanks," James said.

"But don't you think it's time you drove yourself?"

Sheer terror spread across his face. "Me, drive?"

Jairo and the boys laughed. "Come on, kid. If you're old enough to have a girlfriend, you're old enough to drive."

When James returned to the field the next morning, there was a new team manager. James recognized him from his picture on the long wall of pictures outside the front office. It was one of the past team managers. He was a man named Julio Cesar Falcioni who was a goalkeeper for the Argentine national team in 1989, but he looked a lot older in person than his picture. The players were assembled and the new manager was introduced.

"Things are going to be different around here," Falcioni said to the players. "You know why?"

"Because you are new?" One of the players asked.

"No," Falcioni said. "Because you are not *winning.*"

Silence fell upon the squad.

"If I am too hard on you, please let me know. I won't care, but please let me know, so I can make it even harder," he said.

The boys chuckled. Falcioni was a lot funnier than Burruchaga.

"Unless you are winning," the manager continued. "Then and *only then,* will I care. Do we have a deal?"

"YES SIR!" The team shouted.

"Good," he said. "I know how talented you are, I have been watching you from out there for sometime." He pointed to the stands. "Anybody here see me?" He asked.

No one had seen him.

"I didn't think so," he said. "I was disguised as a Fugazzeta salesman."

Everyone laughed. Fugazzetas were the Argentinian pizzas they sold at matches.

"Okay, get to it," he said and the team dispersed. "James!" He said and James stopped and came back. "Yes, coach?"

"I was here when your mother came to sign your contract," Falcioni said.

"Don't tell me," James said. "You were disguised as a desk."

Falcioni laughed and it was a nice laugh.

It reminded him of Juancar's laugh.

"I know how good you are. I want you to shine under me. You have the potential for greatness. I want to help you bring it out."

"Thank you, boss." James felt a knot in his throat.

"I also want to bring your mother down here. She can stay with you." He said. "What do you think?"

James looked at him dumbfounded. "That would be so great!" He said, choking.

"I thought so," Falcioni said. "I promise to make the arrangements. And what are you going to promise to do?"

James grinned. "Win."

Falcioni patted him on the back. "That's exactly what I wanted to hear."

A month later, James became the youngest athlete to play in Argentina's First Division and the first to score a goal when they played against Rosario. Over the course of the year, his mother and sister moved in with him. Falcioni managed to build up James' body naturally, without hormone treatments. He delivered more intense training sessions and it paid off. James scored 10 goals in 50 games and a bunch of great assists. The stands were filled with fans who had heard or read about him and came to see him. James Rodriguez was the kid who could pass brilliantly and score with ease, inside the box or outside of it, facing the goal or with his back to the goal He was a great teammate and everyone loved his winning smile.

The team won and kept winning without stopping. And on December 13, 2009, at La Bombonera Stadium in Buenos Aires, with James' family in attendance, Banfield won the Argentinian League title for the first time in team history. James beamed with joy when he hoisted the league trophy over his head after they had won. It was a great moment for the team. But there was someone missing from the celebration: Daniela. He missed her with all his heart.

Coming off the field after the celebration, he was pinned-down by a reporter.

"James!" A reporter shouted, "A few words please!"

James smiled politely. "My name is Ha-mess," he said correcting him. "That is the name my father gave me."

The reporter apologized and corrected the pronunciation. "You are the youngest player to ever score a goal in Argentina's top division. What are your plans here at Banfield now that you've won the Argentinian League?"

James grinned. He felt a lot different than he did just a few months ago when he was down. He remembered some of the things his agent, Silvio Sandri, the man who brought him to Argentina, told him, just in case any press ever asked him what his plans were for the future: *'If you want to make it to Europe, lay the pipe, James,' he said. 'The pipe that will get you to Europe.'*

"This is the perfect league to keep growing as a player and to jump into European football, which is my dream," James replied.

"Why Europe?" The reporter asked.

"It is where I can be at my best." The reporter wrote down his every word. "What do you do in your spare time?" he asked.

"Besides soccer?"

"Sure," the reporter said.

"I watch as many matches as I can find on TV. And if I can't find any, then I play them on my PlayStation." He flashed the reporter a grin and went into the locker room.

Chapter Twenty

THE GLARING WHITE PEUGEOT swerved around the corner, barely missing a line of parked cars, and rocketed down the hill toward the Palermo neighborhood. James was behind the wheel, and he didn't know what he was doing.

He was halfway home to his apartment when the engine cut out and he thought he was going to die. He fondly called his car *The White Threat,* because it was a snowy white Peugeot 306 and at that moment, it seemed to have a mind of its own. His uncle Andrew had taught him to drive when he was fourteen and he wasn't very good then and he certainly wasn't any better now. It's just that there were so many problems with him taking the bus back and forth to the stadium, that Juancar made him get his license and a car. That was last week.

The Peugeot engine mysteriously cut out while going downhill and James was forced to drift and coast until he finally found some room at the curb and pulled over and parked, tires screeching. He got out and crossed the road to a public telephone booth and dialed-up Juancar, who was visiting.

"Juancar," he said into the phone. "The car died again." He hung up and went back to his car and grabbed his kit bag, locked the car, then started the walk home.

It was already evening and as he walked, he went over what Coach Falcioni said to him. "I know you think you are the fastest man on the team and you are, but I'm telling you right now, you have to go faster."

"But why? I can already outrun everyone I've ever played against," James replied.

"Everyone you played against *here*," the coach said. "I'm not talking about here. I'm talking about Europe. And in Europe they play faster."

"Why are you telling me this?" James asked.

"Because I know I won't be able to keep you here much longer."

"But why?" James asked, worried he had done something wrong.

"Because you are too good for this league, Coffee. You're the best of the best. You're the crack. And the money is not here. The big money is across the sea."

James felt honored. Coach Falcioni was as fair and as honest as they come. If Falcioni said he had to speed it up for Europe, he had to speed it up. He threw the straps of his kit over his shoulders so the bag rested on his back like a daypack. Then he ran. He ran like he had never run before. He ran as fast as he could and pushed it to the limit. And before long, he was home.

And when he opened the door, he got the surprise of his life.

Daniela was standing there in the doorway. She rushed forward and hugged him tight.

"I missed you so much!" She whispered to him.

"Me too," James said. He finally realized they were not alone and looked around the room. Daniela's mother, Lucia, his mother, his sister and his stepfather were all sitting on the couch, watching.

Minutes later, James and Daniela walked hand-in-hand along the river.

James and Daniela were happy to finally be together after all these long months. "While I am here, mama and I are going to see a volleyball match," she said. Her lifelong passion was volleyball, a very popular sport in Argentina.

James felt like it was the best day of his life. Actually, it was one of many more to come.

The bus to Bristol Beach in Mar del Plata was a rough ride on an unfinished road and generally took four hours. There was a series of matches to be played with the local team, but there was also a long, wide stretch of warm beach to be explored.

Halfway through the trip, with the ocean in clear view below, the bus pulled over to the side and stopped. The traffic that was stuck behind the bus, streamed by.

"Why are we stopping?" Jairo said, looking around.

"Letting the cars go by?" James asked as a couple more cars motored by.

Then, curiously, the door up front opened and Falcioni stepped off the bus. Puzzled, James peered out the window and saw a taxi cab parked a short distance away. A man got out of the cab and Falcioni walked over to him and greeted him and they shook hands.

"Who is he talking to?" Someone closer to the front asked.

"It's Mr. Diaz," James said, squinting to see. "The sporting director."

"What's he doing out here? He never comes to Mar Del Plata."

"Coach Falcioni looks nervous," James noted.

Outside, Falcioni and Clyde Diaz, the Banfield sporting director, headed back to the bus and climbed aboard. Falcioni stood behind the Banfield official, who stopped at the head of the aisle.

"Gentlemen, may I have your attention!" Diaz shouted and the bus grew quiet. "Let's all be the first to congratulate James. He was just picked up by Porto. He's going to Lisbon!"

The bus erupted in a crescendo of cheers.

James was surrounded by his team mates and Luchetti the goalkeeper pretended to cut his hair again.

"James, grab your bag!" Diaz continued. "You are coming with me."

James' eyes grew wide and he tried to hide his anxiety.

Jairo saw his friend's fear and draped his arm over the younger man's shoulders. "Don't forget to say goodbye, Jamesito," he said.

James studied his friend, holding back the tears.

Falcioni's shadow fell across James and he looked up at the man who had turned them all into winners. "Congratulations, Coffee. You made it." He stuck out his hand and James took it and stood up. They hugged. "Remember. They go real fast in Europe."

James nodded and walked up the aisle as his team mates slapped his back, shook his hand, and hugged him. When he got to the front of the bus he took one last look at his team, then left and boarded the taxi cab back to Buenos Aires. His days at Banfield were over, he was sold for five million, and he knew what he was going to do the minute he got home.

Ask for Daniela's hand in marriage.

On the day James left for Lisbon, he had the taxi take him to Banfield first to say goodbye to Jairo Patiño. The team had returned the previous day and when he arrived, he found his friend already on the pitch, warming up. They took a walk around the field.

"I was just kidding, you didn't have to come see me," Jairo said, ruffling James' thick black hair. "Not that I'm ever going to see you again."

"I'll see you again. We got a lot of games left to play," James said.

Jairo knew he wouldn't, but he pretended to believe him. "Sure, I know," he said. "You uh — you take care of Daniela, okay?"

"Promise," James relied.

"The two of you — you are good for each other," Jairo said. "She comes from a soccer family. She already knows the life. The loneliness. The despair of marrying a soccer legend. You just can't buy that kind of suffering," he joked.

"Can you keep a secret?" James asked.

"Certainly," he replied.

"I asked her to — marry me."

Jairo's face lit up and he hugged his friend. They said their goodbyes and James got back in the cab and rode to the airport. A few hours later, when the plane took off, he said goodbye to Argentina. He was on his way to Portugal.

And his first thought when he got off the plane in Lisbon, was how warm it was. And for that, he was grateful.

Chapter Twenty-One

PORTO WAS ONE OF THE TOP 3 TEAMS in Portugal, with Benfica, and Sporting Lisbon. The team played at the *Estádio do Dragão,* home of the Blue-and-Whites, the Dragons of Porto. The stadium was named after the mythical creature that topped the team's logo and was inaugurated in 2003 with a match against Barcelona, where Leo Messi made his professional debut. Porto won 2-0.

At his presentation, James wore the blue and white shirt with the FCP dragon logo of his new team and felt happy and proud. But the beginning wasn't inspiring. In James' first year there, he wasn't a starter and he did not score a single goal for over five months. The dry spell ended only in December.

But he wasn't lonely. He was happy to have two friends on the Porto squad. His old friend from Envigado, Fredy Guarin was thrilled to meet him when he arrived.

"What took you, Jamesito?" Guarin asked. "I haven't seen you since I was smart enough to get myself to Europe first!"

James chuckled and bumped fists. "I used to tell my mother I wished I'd gone with you to Boca, now I'm glad I didn't."

"How is she?" Guarin asked.

"She's fine, though she didn't want me to come here. She wanted me to go to Benfica," James said. Pilar was a Benfica fan.

Guarin chuckled. "That's the problem. Your mother is a bigger soccer fan than you are," he said. "Anyway, you're going to have to get used to me. We're roommates. Along with this useless striker," he quipped, jerking his thumb toward the man standing next to him. He was about five years older than James, slightly shorter, with rugged features and long dark hair held off his face with a black headband.

The man with dark hair shoved out his hand and James shook it. "Radamel," he said.

"Falcao?" James asked. "It is so nice to meet you!"

"Yeah, nice to meet you too," Falcao replied. "We have something in common."

"Oh yeah? What's that?" James asked, surprised.

"Our fathers played together."

"What?!" James said. "Where?!"

"Deportes Tolima!"

That's when the head coach, Andre Villas-Boas started the practice and everyone took the field, leaving James still trying to process what Falcao had just told him. "Are you kidding?!" He shouted after the striker.

Falcao happily shook his head. "Get out here! I need you!"

James raced out on the field. And when the trio from Columbia worked together, Villas-Boas, watching from the sideline, thought it was like instant magic. "This is better than I expected," he said to his assistants. "James is the perfect addition to Guarin and Falcao." Villas-Boas had just moved up to head coach after assisting Jose Mourinho for six years. Now it was his turn to show what he could do.

James scored a goal for Porto in a friendly against

Ajax and by the time the end of the year rolled around on December 15, James took the field against CSKA Sofia in the Europa League and scored his first goal in European soccer. Porto won 3-1. He had earned his place on the squad and the trio of James, Falcao, and Guarin became known as *The Trident.*

A week later, on Christmas Eve, he married the love of his life, Daniela Ospina.

The next two years were busy for James. Porto won the Portuguese League title as well as the Europa League trophy with James scoring six goals and eight assists in 24 appearances. He took some time off to play in the FIFA U20 World Cup for his beloved Columbia for the first time, scored five goals, and suddenly everyone in his home country knew his name, including *El Pibe* himself, his fellow Colombian, Carlos Valderrama, the man who had more caps than anyone else in the history of Los Cafeteros.

"Colombia does not need another El Pibe," Valderrama said. "James is doing very well in that position."

By the end of the 2011-2012 season, James and his team had won the Portuguese League title again and James personally won the Golden Ball award, the youngest player to ever receive the award.

But that success was nowhere near as exciting as the news Daniela delivered to him that September day in 2012 out on the field.

The first team was warming up. James' new agent, Jorge Mendes, watched from the stands. Falcao saw her first. She was already halfway out to them, still dressed in her volleyball team uniform, walking briskly toward them.

"Excuse me, James?" Falcao asked.

"Yes?" James replied.

"Why is your wife coming this way?"

James looked and saw Daniela walking briskly toward him.

Everyone on the field stopped what they were doing and watched as she took their star team mate in her arms and whispered something in his ear.

Before he could say a word, turned, waved happily to the team, then strode off without looking back.

"What's up?" Fredy Guarin wanted to know.

James faced his team mates, tears streaming down his face. "I'm pregnant!" He shouted. The whole team burst out laughing, then erupted in wild cheers.

James was given the number 10 shirt that season and while his fellow Colombians, Fredy Guarin, Radamel Falcao, and Hulk, the Brazilian forward, had left for other teams, he became a regular starter for the first time. He led the team to its third consecutive Portuguese League title and all in, managed to rack up a total of 32 goals in 107 games as well as eight awards. He became one of the up and coming young star players in Europe.

On May 24, 2013, Jorge Mendes announced James Rodriguez, 21, was moving to AS Monaco, for more than $50 million. James and Daniela both agreed they wanted their baby to be born at home, so they boarded a plane for Medellin and on the 29th of May, their daughter, Salome, was born.

Both families gathered around the long dinner table in Medellin. Pilar, Juancar, Lucia, Daniela's mother, David, her brother, Daniela with Salome in her arms, and James.

"Okay everybody," James announced. "I have a surprise. Mama, don't look." Pilar gave him a disapproving look.

"Does this mean I have to go to confession in the morning?" She asked and everyone laughed.

"No, nothing like that, mama," James said and proudly rolled up his sleeve and revealed a brand new tattoo on his right forearm. It was one name written fancy blue script: SALOME.

Everyone applauded.

"You know, that doesn't come off," Juancar joked.

"That's why I did it. Now she will be with me for the rest of my life and hers and she will always know that she has only one father. Me."

He looked to Juancar, then to his mother, and Pilar burst out crying. She got up and went over to him and took her son in her arms.

"Okay okay, I love you too mama," he said, consoling the woman who had consoled him his entire life. "I love you. Both of you. Not because I am your son, but because you raised me. You are my mother and you, Juancar, are the only father I have ever known."

"You are my son," Juancar said, his eyes welling with tears.

"And you are my father," James said. He went over and hugged him. "Thank you for raising me and giving me the love and the courage and the hope and the strength to raise my own child," he said. "There's one thing I know," he said, kissing Salome's name on his arm. "This arm will always be there for her. Just like yours was for me."

James was at AS Monaco for less than a year and scored 10 goals in 38 games. Real Madrid began looking at him. When his agent told him that Real Madrid was playing in Munich, Germany, he drove his sports car over 600 miles to watch the semi-final of the Champions League between Madrid and Bayern Munich at the Allianz Arena. After the game, he met his hero, Cristiano Ronaldo, for the first time. He had his picture taken with him.

Then *Los Cafeteros* head coach Jose Pekerman asked him to captain the Colombian national team for the upcoming World Cup. He wore the prestigious number 10 jersey, and took his team to Brazil in 2014, where he scored 6 goals, won the Golden Boot, and finally, the Puskas Award for Goal of the Year, the goal against Uruguay, the country he saw through binoculars when he gazed out his apartment window in Buenos Aires.

The goal he first made as a kid, on the streets of his beloved Ibague.

Without looking. His back to the goal.

Turning around and sending the ball swiftly into the net.

Because he was born upside down, with eyes in the back of his head.

JAMES RODRIGUEZ AWARDS AND HONORS

Porto

- UEFA Europa League: 2010–11
- Primeira Liga: 2010–11, 2011–12, 2012–13
- Taça de Portugal: 2010–11
- Supertaça Cândido de Oliveira: 2010, 2011, 2012

Real Madrid

- UEFA Champions League: 2015–16
- UEFA Super Cup: 2014
- FIFA Club World Cup: 2014

International Colombia

- Toulon Tournament: 2011
- Copa América: Third place 2016

Individual

- Youngest Foreigner Player ever to score in the Argentine Primera Division (age 17)
- Best Player Toulon Tournament: 2011[150]
- LPFP Primeira Liga Breakthrough Player of the Year: 2011–12
- SJPF Player of the Month: August 2012, September 2012
- Record Team of the Year: 2012
- O Jogo Team of the Year: 2012 2013
- Portuguese Golden Ball: 2012
- Ligue 1 Assist Leader: 2013–14
- UNFP Ligue 1 XI: 2013–14
- AS Monaco Player of the Year: 2013–14
- Globe Revelation Player : 2014
- FIFA World Cup Golden Boot: 2014
- FIFA World Cup All-Star Team: 2014
- FIFA World Cup Dream Team: 2014
- FIFA World Cup 2014 Goal of the Tournament: 1–0 (2–0) vs. Uruguay
- FIFA Puskás Award: 2014
- La Liga Team of the Season: 2014–15
- LFP Best Midfielder: 2014–15

- UEFA Team of the Year: 2015
- Facebook FA La Liga Best Goal: 2016

The Flea – The Amazing Story of Leo Messi

By Michael Part

The captivating story of soccer legend Lionel Messi, from his first touch at age five in the streets of Rosario, Argentina, to his first goal on the Camp Nou pitch in Barcelona, Spain. *The Flea* tells the amazing story of a boy who was born to play the beautiful game and destined to become the world's greatest soccer player. The best-selling book by Michael Part is a must read for every soccer fan!

Ages 9 and up

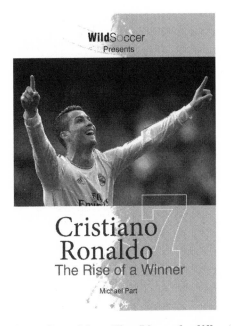

WildSoccer
Presents

Cristiano
Ronaldo
The Rise of a Winner

Michael Part

Cristiano Ronaldo – The Rise of a Winner

By Michael Part

Cristiano Ronaldo: The Rise of a Winner is the gripping life story of a boy who rose from the streets of Madeira to become one of the greatest soccer players ever. This heartfelt, stirring tale chronicles Ronaldo's road to glory, a journey that made him the man he is today.

Michael Part is the author of *The Flea: The Amazing Story of Leo Messi*, *The Pope Who Loves Soccer*, and the Disney classic *A Kid in King Arthur's Court*.

Ages 9 and up

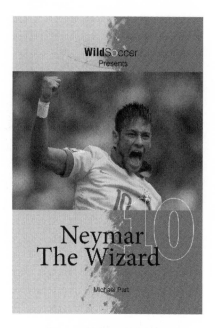

Neymar The Wizard

By Michael Part

Neymar The Wizard is the fascinating coming of age story of Neymar Junior, the skinny kid from Mogi Das Cruzes in Brazil, who has been called the next Pelé. Neymar has taken Brazil and the world by storm and continues to inspire millions around the world with his talent, his open heart, and his engaging smile. Following the international bestsellers, *The Flea: The Amazing Story of Leo Messi* and *Ronaldo, The Rise of a Winner* by Michael Part, *Neymar The Wizard* is a heartwarming and emotional story about a father and son who, against all odds, made the journey from the verge of poverty to international stardom through love, conviction, and belief.

Michael Part is also the critically acclaimed author of *The Pope Who Loves Soccer,* the first account on Pope Francis coming of age and his lifelong love to soccer.

Ages 9 and up

Balotelli – The Untold Story

By Michael Part

Talented, unique, and always on the edge, this is the story of *Mario Balotelli's* journey from near death as an infant to becoming one of the world's best known strikers. Balotelli's story is one of triumph over personal and racial challenges, and his struggle to find his own true identity.

Michael Part is the best-selling author of *The Flea - The Amazing Story of Leo Messi, Cristiano Ronaldo - the Rise of a Winner, Neymar - The Wizard,* and *The Pope Who Loves Soccer.* His books are published in more than 30 countries worldwide.

Ages 9 and up

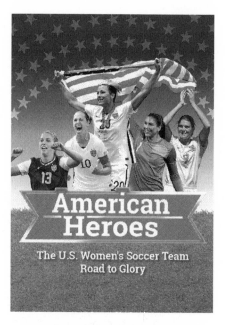

American Heroes –
The U.S. Women's Soccer Team Road to Glory

By Noah Davis & Rick Leddy

American Heroes is the amazing story of the United States' Women's National Soccer Team: the good, the bad, and the ugly, the past, the present, and the future. Come along for the ride. It's a tale filled with soaring wins, crushing losses, trophies, gold medals, and a few songs along the way.

Noah Davis is the author of The World's Best Soccer Strikers and Rick Leddy is the author of LeBron James The King of the Game.

Ages 9 and up

HAVE YOU READ THE FIRST BOOK?
GET IT NOW!

THE WILD SOCCER BUNCH
BOOK 1
KEVIN the Star Striker

When the last of the snow has finally melted, soccer season starts!

Kevin the Star Striker and the *Wild Soccer Bunch* rush to their field. They have found that Mickey the bulldozer and his gang, the *Unbeatables*, have taken over. Kevin and his friends challenge the *Unbeatables* to the biggest game of their lives.

Can the *Wild Soccer Bunch* defeat the *Unbeatables*, or will they lose their field of dreams forever? Can they do what no team has done before?

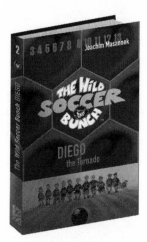

THE WILD SOCCER BUNCH
BOOK 2
DIEGO the Tornado

Fabio, the son of a famous Brazilian soccer player, wants to join the *Wild Soccer Bunch*. But Fabio's father has other plans. He makes his son play for the *Furies,* one of the best youth club teams in the country. The *Wild Soccer Bunch* is devastated, but Diego has a plan. He turns the *Wild Soccer Bunch* into a club team and challenges the *Furies* to a game! Can the *Wild Soccer Bunch* survive the game? Can their friendship endure the test?

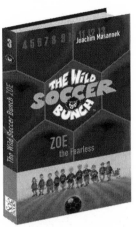

THE WILD SOCCER BUNCH
BOOK 3
ZOE the Fearless

Zoe is ten and soccer crazy. She spends each day dreaming of becoming the first woman to play for the U.S. Men's National Soccer Team. Her dad believes in her dream, and encourages her to join the *Wild Soccer Bunch*. Even though Zoe would be the only girl on the team, she knows she could be their best player. But the *Wild Bunch* is not open-minded when it comes to welcoming new teammates, especially when they are girls...

Zoe's dad has a plan. He organizes a birthday tournament and invites the *Wild Bunch*. They present Zoe with a pair of red high heels, expecting her to make a fool of herself during the tournament. Zoe gladly accepts her gift. She wears the heels during the biggest game of her life, and proves that she's got what it takes to be a wild, winning member of the *Wild Soccer Bunch*.

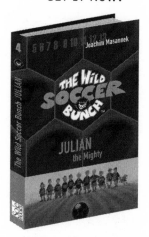

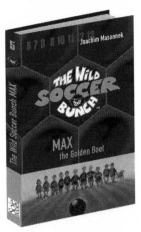

Made in the USA
Columbia, SC
29 November 2018